THE WORLD OF

History
Revision

Anna Smith

Contents

Off with their heads!

The Tudor period has something for everyone.

If you like action and adventure, then how about the voyages of John Cabot, who sailed into the unknown and ended up 'discovering' Newfoundland in Canada? Or how about Sir Francis Drake, an Elizabethan sailor, who raided Spanish treasure ships and helped to protect England from the Spanish Armada?

If you like stories of power and passion, then look at King Henry VIII. He changed the religion of his entire country. Do you think that this might have been just to be able to marry a new wife, Anne Boleyn?

Are we a little overdressed for dinner?

If you like 'real life' stories, then what about the early lives of the princesses, Mary and Elizabeth? They were both children of King Henry VIII. Mary was brought up as a favourite princess until Henry divorced her mother, Catherine. Elizabeth then became the favourite child until Henry had her mother, Anne, executed, and she was in turn expected to stand aside in favour of a new little brother.

Here are some of the most important kings and queens from the Tudor period.

- **Henry VII** (reigned 1485–1509): the first Tudor monarch and founder of the dynasty, he defeated the Yorkist King Richard III at the battle of Bosworth. He married Elizabeth of York – the niece of the man he had killed to become king. He enjoyed music, gambling and building palaces.

- **Henry VIII** (reigned 1509–47): son of Henry VII. Henry wanted a son to rule after him and married three times before a son was born. In total, he married six times! When he became king, England was part of the Roman Catholic Church, but Henry took England away from the Pope's control. He had many hobbies, from hunting to music and songwriting.

- **Edward VI** (reigned 1547–53): the only son of Henry VIII. He was just a child when he became king, and he died very young. His government tried to make England a very Protestant country. Edward enjoyed reading about battles and writing Greek.

- **Mary I** (reigned 1553–58): the elder daughter of Henry VIII. She was a Catholic and returned the English Church to the control of the Pope. She was very musical.

- **Elizabeth I** (reigned 1558–1603): younger daughter of Henry VIII. She made England Protestant again. During her reign, England became an enemy of Catholic Spain, and Elizabeth fought against Philip II's navy (the <u>Spanish Armada</u>). She was well educated and spoke several languages.

Tudorgram

The following words are muddled-up versions of some of the words and names found in this chapter. Can you unscramble them?

1 BY NEON LANE	
2 AIRMAN HAS PADS	
3 HAZEL BITE	
4 RHEYN	

All change!

The early <u>Stuart period</u> deserves better attention than it often receives. This was a time of new ideas and customs, of huge changes in government and plots, plagues and of city fires. It also was a time when it was difficult for a monarch to keep the throne and where supporters quickly changed sides. Charles I was executed by his own <u>Parliament</u>, and James II was <u>deposed</u> by his daughter and son-in-law.

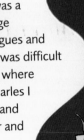

Kings and Protectors

- **James I (reigned 1603–25):** already King James VI of Scotland when he became King of England in 1603. He wanted to unite the two countries but did not succeed. His reign is perhaps most famous for the Gunpowder Plot of 1605, when a group of Catholics plotted to blow up the Houses of Parliament with James inside.

- **Charles I (reigned 1625–49):** Charles was not brought up to become king, but his elder brother, Henry, died of typhoid at the age of 18. Many historians feel that Charles was a weak king and that his mistakes brought about the Civil War. He did, however, attempt to make the royal court more moral than it was under his father, James I.

- **Republic:** England was a republic from 1649 to 1660. At first, England was ruled by Parliament, but in 1653, Oliver Cromwell, commander of the army, became Lord Protector of England. He held this post until his death in 1658 (when his son briefly took over). Cromwell did not want to be king and refused the crown when it was offered to him.

- **Charles II (reigned 1660–85):** Charles was made king in 1660 in the <u>Restoration</u>. Parliament dated his reign from his father's death in 1649 to show that they felt the Protectorate had not been a real government. Charles tried to bring the different sides together. For example, he passed the Act of Indemnity and Oblivion, which pardoned people who had fought against his father, with just a few exceptions (such as those who signed Charles I's death warrant). He became a Catholic on his deathbed.

- **James II (reigned 1685–8):** the younger brother of Charles II. As a Catholic, James II wanted to push Catholic rights forward, but he could not get rid of the acts that stopped Catholics having equal rights to Protestants in England. He survived a rebellion in 1685 from the Protestant Duke of Monmouth, the illegitimate son of Charles II. In 1688, however, James was deposed by William of Orange, who was married to his daughter, Mary.

The first political party

Charles II's brother, James, was a Catholic, and some people wanted him excluded from the <u>succession</u>. They felt that they would have to limit royal authority in many ways to get this done. This was known as the 'exclusion crisis'. The opposition members of Parliament formed a group and ran election campaigns to support candidates. They became known as 'Whigs'. They failed to get James excluded from succession but set up the first English political party. (Very soon after, the supporters of the King set up their own party, which became known as the 'Tories').

The truth about the Stuarts

Write **true** or **false** in the box next to each statement.

1 James I was already King of France before he became King of England.

2 The Gunpowder Plot involved a group of Protestants who tried to blow up Parliament.

3 Charles I had an older brother called Richard.

4 James II was Charles I's son.

5 Charles II became a Catholic on his deathbed.

KEY FACTS

⬆ During this period, there were many changes in the relationship between the <u>monarchy</u> and Parliament, which wanted more say in how the country was run.

➡ Ireland, Scotland and Wales were important in deciding events in England. For example, the Scots were crucial in the outcome of the Civil War. Likewise, English rulers became involved in the internal affairs of these countries. For example, many attempts were made to strengthen the crown's power in Ireland.

⬇ Religion was extremely important to many, and people often took political action based on their religious views.

⬆ Charles II tried to change the Church of England to make it more popular with Puritans. Although he was not successful, he worked hard to protect <u>nonconformists</u>.

➡ Both the Great Plague (1665) and Great Fire of London (1666) took place during the reign of Charles II.

⬆ The 'Royal Society for the Promotion of Natural Knowledge' was founded in 1660 at the <u>accession to the throne</u> of Charles II. This society aimed to improve scientific understanding, and members included many famous scientists. It helped push forward the study of science and still exists today.

• TOP TIPS •

A significant event is something that has a special meaning or importance – it often has a major impact on history. An example is the setting up of the first English political parties, which happened during the Stuart period.

Exciting times!

Many of us don't know much about the period after the Glorious Revolution, when William III and Mary II became joint rulers in 1689. However, it was a very exciting period, full of personal tragedy for rulers, battles, rebellions and big changes in politics.

The first prime minister?

In 1722, Robert Walpole became First Lord of the Treasury. He controlled the government until 1742 and was probably the first prime minister. He wouldn't have called himself this though; back then the term would have been an insult, because it described one man who took too much power for himself.

Banks and bankruptcy

The Bank of England was founded in 1694. The Tories felt it was too much in the hands of the Whigs, so they set up the South Sea Company as a rival in 1711. This did really well at first, and many people invested a lot of money. Suddenly, however, the value of shares fell sharply, and many people lost a lot of money. This was called the bursting of the 'South Sea Bubble'.

War!

One of William III's first actions was to get England involved in wars against France. Two major wars happened – the Nine Years War (also known as King William's War) 1688–97 and the War of the Spanish Succession 1701–14. These helped to make Britain much more powerful in Europe – a real rival to powerful France – but they also cost a lot of money.

Methodists

In 1738, John Wesley, a clergyman of the Church of England, began preaching 'methodist' ideas. He felt the Church of England had lost its excitement about the good news of Jesus and he wanted to spread the message. He was seen as very radical, and his supporters had to set up a separate 'church' – the Methodist Church. (The name comes from the 'method' of studying the Bible and exploring the Christian life developed by John's brother Charles.)

Whigs and Tories

In the last chapter, we saw how the political parties – the Whigs and Tories – were set up. In fact, both names were first used as insults. 'Whig' is an insulting word for a Scottish Protestant, and Tory is a name for an Irish bandit.

Setting the date!

Decide on a date for each of these events and then write them down in chronological order.

Accession of Queen Anne	1702-1714
Accession of George I	1714-1727
Accession of George II	1114-1127
First Jacobite Rebellion	1715
Glorious Revolution	1689-1694
Second Jacobite Rebellion	1745
'Start' of Methodism	1738
Start of Nine Years War	1688-1697
Walpole becomes first Prime Minister (Lord Treasurer)	1722-1742

KEY FACTS

Queens and kings

⬆ **William and Mary:** joint rulers at first (1689–94), then William ruled on his own (1694–1702). They became rulers after the Glorious Revolution (1688), when James II was deposed in favour of his Protestant daughter. William was a Dutch prince and a relation of James II. His wife, Mary, was the daughter of James II. This meant that she was partly responsible for deposing her own father!

➡ **Queen Anne** (1702–14): desperately wanted an <u>heir</u>. She was pregnant 17 times, but all the children, except one, were miscarried, <u>stillborn</u> or died when they were babies. Her one surviving son, William, Duke of Gloucester, died at the age of 11. Anne carried on the war against France, which had started in 1702. The most famous battle of this time was the Battle of Blenheim. This was fought by British, Austrian, German and Dutch troops against the French and Bavarians. The British were led by John Churchill, an ancestor of Winston Churchill. Anne's reign also saw the Act of Union between England and Scotland (1707).

⬇ **George I** (1714–27): a distant cousin of Queen Anne. George came from Hanover, in Germany, and spoke very little English. He was the first 'Hanoverian' king. He often supported the Whigs, because he felt that the Tories were secret supporters of the Jacobites (who wanted to put the Stuarts back on the throne). The first Jacobite Rebellion took place during his reign (1715).

⬆ **George II** (1727–60): son of George I. He carried on supporting the Whigs. The second Jacobite Rebellion took place during his reign (1745).

· TOP TIPS ·

You will really impress if you can demonstrate a good knowledge of this period. A lot of people have a big 'gap' in their understanding of history between 1688 and the Victorian period.

Test your knowledge 1

This assessment aims to help you feel confident about some of the key events and people of the period.

Task 1

Write the letter from the corresponding statement in column two into the box in column one.

1	Battle of Bosworth, 1485	☐	A	Second of two rebellions that tried to put the Stuarts back on the throne
2	Break with Rome, 1530s	☐	B	Foiled Catholic plot to blow up the Houses of Parliament
3	Reign of Edward VI, 1547–53	☐	C	Start of the rule of the Stuart dynasty in England. England and Scotland have the same monarch
4	Reign of Mary I, 1553–8	☐	D	James II is deposed. William and Mary become joint monarchs. Bill of Rights means a lot of changes in the power of the monarchy and Parliament
5	Elizabethan 'settlement', 1558 to early 1560s	☐	E	This man is often called England's first prime minister
6	Spanish Armada, 1588	☐	F	England fights a large Spanish invasion force
7	Accession of James I, 1603	☐	G	Henry Tudor beats Richard III in battle and becomes Henry VII
8	Gunpowder Plot, 1605	☐	H	First of two rebellions that try to put the Stuarts back on the throne
9	The English Republic, 1649–60	☐	I	During the reign of this child of Henry VIII, the government tried to make England very Protestant
10	The Restoration, 1660	☐	J	After the civil war and the execution of Charles I, England became a republic. Oliver Cromwell ruled England for some of this time
11	The Glorious Revolution, 1688–9	☐	K	Henry VIII splits England from the Catholic Church
12	Act of Union, 1707	☐	L	Elizabeth I makes the English church Protestant again
13	First Jacobite Rebellion, 1715	☐	M	During the reign of this child of Henry VIII, the English church returned to the Catholic faith
14	Robert Walpole becomes First Lord of the Treasury, 1722	☐	N	The monarchy is restored when Charles II is made king
15	Second Jacobite Rebellion, 1745	☐	O	England and Scotland are united formally

(15 marks)

Task 2

Write down the names of two of the four dynasties (ruling families) that were in power during the years 1485–1750.

....

(4 marks)

Task 3

In order, write down the names of all the monarchs and rulers from 1485 to 1750.

....

....

....

....

(6 marks)

(Total 25 marks)

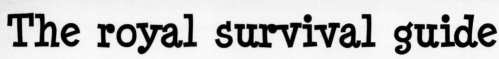

The royal survival guide

If you were king, how would you want your life to be? You would probably want luxury, lots of servants, nice food and beautiful palaces with constant feasts and parties. You certainly wouldn't want to spend all your childhood and teenage years in terrible danger, before becoming a ruler in even greater danger.

Henry Tudor was part of an important family, the Lancastrians, which fought with another family, the Yorkists, to rule England in the Wars of the Roses. When Henry was young, he was a prisoner of the Yorkists for a time. He later escaped to Europe, where he was kept safe by the Duke of Brittany. Unfortunately, Richard III – a Yorkist – made a deal with the Duke of Brittany, and Henry had to escape to the court of the King of France. In the end, the King of France gave Henry money and an army to invade England. In 1485, Henry beat Richard III at the Battle of Bosworth.

Although Henry had defeated Richard, he had lots of problems. Put yourself in Henry's shoes and imagine the following:

I feel rather full all of a sudden

- You hardly know anybody, have been living abroad for years, don't know the royal palaces and have never been to London.
- You don't know much about being a king. Most kings are raised at the royal court, but you spent most of your life as a prisoner or on the run – not great training for ruling a country!
- Not everyone wants you as king. Although you had some English supporters, many leading <u>nobles</u> fought against you at the Battle of Bosworth.
- The French gave you lots of support at Bosworth. Some people, including the French, expect you to do whatever the French want, which won't be popular in England.
- England has had years of <u>civil war</u>. The important families have big private armies, which they use to depose kings. No one can be trusted. People are happy to change sides if they think it will help them do well.

How do you rate your chances of survival? Will you be desposed like Henry VI (a previous king) or killed in battle like Richard III? Perhaps you should just give up. But if you don't, how will you keep yourself safe and bring peace to your country?

Henry Tudor didn't give up. Not only did he survive, he also started one of the most famous ruling families ever in England – the Tudors.

Money

Henry knew it was important to be rich because he could throw grand parties to impress people. He could also pay for soldiers if he needed to fight. Henry was good at raising money, and by the end of his reign he had an income of more than £100 000 a year – a lot of money at the time.

Marriages

- Henry married Elizabeth – the daughter of a previous Yorkist king, Edward IV. This meant he could say he was bringing the two families together.
- Henry married his daughter Margaret to the King of Scotland. This meant that Scotland stopped supporting his enemies, such as Perkin Warbeck.
- Henry married his son Arthur to Catherine, daughter of the King and Queen of what we know as Spain. This gave him important allies in Europe. When Arthur died, Henry VII made sure that Catherine was engaged to his younger son Henry instead.

Tudorsearch

The wordsearch below contains 20 things that have been mentioned in this chapter. How many can you find? Circle them on the grid and cross them out in the list below.

J	P	E	R	K	I	N	W	A	R	B	E	C	K	M
S	E	Q	E	I	Y	T	A	H	X	A	O	A	H	A
V	C	Y	D	N	I	F	R	A	N	C	E	T	L	R
A	I	O	E	G	R	E	S	Y	R	N	E	H	A	G
P	V	R	F	G	Z	Y	O	T	T	N	F	E	N	A
O	I	K	T	E	M	H	F	H	D	E	G	R	C	R
E	L	I	Z	A	B	E	T	H	E	S	S	I	A	E
M	W	S	S	H	E	E	H	S	P	A	I	N	S	T
D	A	T	U	K	G	S	E	C	O	P	M	E	T	D
E	R	S	P	Y	O	H	R	O	S	E	N	R	R	T
M	S	S	E	E	R	R	O	T	E	I	E	O	I	R
O	U	I	S	L	L	T	S	L	E	T	L	E	A	O
N	Y	T	W	H	B	N	E	A	A	R	R	H	N	I
E	R	L	I	Q	S	O	S	N	S	A	P	I	M	H
Y	M	B	U	R	G	U	N	D	Y	I	A	R	M	Y

Perkin Warbeck ✓   Spain   Catherine   Simnel   Scotland
Burgundy   Wars of the Roses   King   Nobles   Margaret
Elizabeth   Civil war   Depose   Henry   Lancastrian
Yorkist   Money ✓   Army   Spy   France

• TOP TIPS •

If you are asked how Henry VII made himself secure as king, you should make sure that you talk about a wide range of different topics. Showing that you know that lots of factors were involved demonstrates good understanding.

KEY FACTS

Nobles

⬆ Henry passed laws so that nobles were only allowed to have their own private armies if they had permission from the king. If they were caught with an illegal army, they were fined a massive amount of money.

➡ Henry had a good spy system, which meant he was able to find out if people were plotting against him.

Margaret of Burgundy

⬆ Margaret of Burgundy was the sister of Richard III, the man that Henry had killed at the Battle of Bosworth. She wanted to get rid of Henry as

soon as she could. To do this, she supported two men who claimed to be members of the Yorkist family Lambert Simnel and Perkin Warbeck.

➡ Lambert Simnel invaded England in 1487, and Henry had to fight him at the Battle of Stoke.

⬆ Perkin Warbeck stayed at Margaret's court in Europe for so long that Henry had to stop all English merchants from trading with her for three years to make her send Warbeck away. Warbeck then went to other rulers of Europe, such as the King of Scotland. Henry had to make lots of treaties with them to stop them from supporting Warbeck. In the end, Warbeck was taken prisoner and executed.

All for love?

In 1521, Henry VIII published a book called *Assertio Septem Sacramentorum (In Defence of the Seven Sacraments)* in response to Martin Luther's ideas (see chapter 'A monk changes Europe'). The book defended Catholic doctrine and the papacy itself. As a reward, Henry was given the title 'Defender of the Faith' by the Pope. Henry seemed a loyal servant of the Catholic Church and papacy.

Anne Boleyn

Catherine of Aragon

Just a few years later, however, Henry VII created the Church of England and brought about the 'Break with Rome'. He announced that kings of England (not the Popes) were, and always had been, head of the Church in England – and that he was rightfully Supreme Head of the Church in England. Although probably never a Protestant, Henry did appoint some bishops with Protestant sympathies. He also allowed some things that pleased Protestants, such as the <u>Dissolution of the Monasteries</u>.

So why did Henry do this? Here are some possible arguments.

- Maybe Henry broke with Rome because he liked Protestant ideas. Henry fancied himself an expert on <u>theology</u> and did like some of the ideas of the Protestants, such as their emphasis on royal power. If he was so keen on all the new ideas, though, why didn't he make his new Church more Protestant? His Church even carried on burning Protestants (such as John Lambert in 1538).

- Perhaps Henry's break with Rome was because he thought his country was already becoming Protestant. Some people certainly supported Protestant ideas, but much of the country was very attached to the old beliefs. For instance, many people still went on <u>pilgrimages</u>. And anyway, was Henry VIII really the sort of monarch who did what his people wanted?

Henry VIII

- Some historians argue that a lot of corruption existed in the Church, which made people dislike priests and the whole Catholic Church. On the other hand, much evidence suggests that priests weren't that unpopular. And would Henry really change the Church because people didn't like priests?

- Henry really wanted a male heir to succeed him. His wife Catherine of Aragon had only given him a girl, Mary, and she was now too old to have more children. Henry had met and fallen in love with Anne Boleyn, one of Catherine's ladies in waiting, but Anne wouldn't become his mistress – she wanted marriage. This was a chance for Henry to marry the woman he loved and get a <u>legitimate</u> heir. He tried to get his marriage to Catherine annulled ('Key Facts' on p.15), but the Pope had to give permission and wouldn't, or couldn't, agree. This might have been because Charles V, Catherine's nephew, was very powerful in Europe. So perhaps the only way for Henry to get his divorce was to break with Rome. Would Henry, however, really do that just to get an heir?

- Perhaps Henry didn't aim to break with Rome but just wanted to attack the Church so that the Pope would give in. He started taking power away from the Pope bit by bit. Perhaps Henry and his advisers soon realised where they were heading and how much power they could get, so they carried on. Would Henry, however, really do all this just for power?

I am ...

Read each description and decide who it is talking about. (At least some of each description is in this chapter.)

1 Keen collector of clocks. Holy Roman Emperor and King of Spain. Nephew of Catherine of Aragon	
2 Suffered from gout. Serial womaniser. King of England	*Henry the VIII*
3 Very religious. Born in Spain. Widow of Prince Arthur and first wife of Henry VIII	*Catherine of Aragon*
4 Possibly a Protestant. Reputed to have had an extra finger. Her sister, Mary, had previously had an affair with the king. Second wife of Henry VIII	*Anne Boleyn*

KEY FACTS

Divorce?

⬆ People often talk about Henry VIII wanting to *divorce* Catherine of Aragon, but divorce wasn't allowed in the Catholic Church. Instead, Henry wanted to argue that his marriage to Catherine had been illegal because she had previously been married to his brother Arthur. Henry argued that this was unbiblical and that he wasn't properly married to Catherine. In this situation, the marriage could be *annulled*.

Katherine Parr

Jane Seymour

Break with Rome?

➡ Most people think the break with Rome took place in 1534, when the Act of Supremacy was passed and recognised Henry as Supreme Head of the Church. This was a very important act, but many acts of Parliament in the previous years had already taken away much of the Pope's powers. Not until 1536 was the Act Against Papal Authority passed. This stated clearly that the Pope had no authority at all in England.

• TOP TIPS •

When you are writing an answer about causes, say what you think was the most important cause, and why you think this.

Different views of Henry VIII

⬆ Some historians argue that Henry VIII was a very strong king who knew his own mind and did exactly what he wanted. Others, however, believe that he was actually quite weak and easily manipulated by those around him.

Catherine Howard

Anne of Cleves

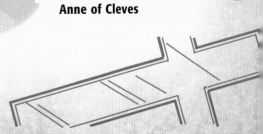

Bloody Mary?

In the sixteenth century, it was very dangerous to hold different religious beliefs to the people in charge, because you could be put into prison or even killed.

In 1553, the Protestant King Edward VI died, and his Catholic sister, Mary, became queen. Mary I wanted to make England a Catholic country again. Almost 300 people were killed because they were Protestants. Many were ordinary people, who were killed by being burnt at the stake. This meant that they were tied to a pole (called a stake) and bundles of wood (called faggots) were put around the pole. The executioner set light to the faggots, and the victim was burnt to death. This took place in public.

Here is a description of the death of a priest, John Laurence, in 1555. It is a summary of a description in a book written by John Foxe. (The picture shows Laurence being burnt in his chair.)

Death of John Laurence

The next day, 29th of March, John Laurence was brought to Colchester. His legs had been injured with the heavy irons he wore in prison. Because he had been so badly treated, his body was very weak, so he was not able to walk and had to be carried to the fire in a chair. He was consumed with fire sitting in this chair.

Mary I has a bad reputation among some historians, partly because of deaths like these. She is often known as 'Bloody Mary', because she was seen as being so bloodthirsty. However, some historians think that Mary I does not deserve this nickname.

Do you think that Mary I deserves her 'bloody' reputation? Look at these arguments and see what you decide.

'Yes, Mary I does deserve her bad reputation'

• Mary I executed a lot more heretics than was normal in England. She burnt about 280 people. All four other Tudor rulers only burnt 111 people between them.

• Mary I's burnings took place in a very short space of time – just a couple of years. This makes the numbers even more shocking.

'No, Mary I does not deserve her bad reputation'

• Foxe, who wrote about Mary I's cruelty, was a Protestant. He also wrote his book in the reign of Mary's Protestant sister Elizabeth, so he might have been trying to make Mary look bad.

• At the time, many people believed it was right to kill **heretics**. For instance, many heretics were executed in Spain at this time.

Mary matters

Answer these questions about Mary I.

1	About how many Protestants were burned under Mary I's rule?	280 people
2	How many heretics were killed under the other Tudor rulers?	111 people between them
3	A heretic is a person whose religious beliefs are thought to be right. True or false?	
4	Whom did Mary I marry?	Philip of Spain
5	Who led a rebellion against Mary I in 1554?	Wyatt's
6	How much better off financially was the monarchy because of Mary I's changes to the way government raised money?	

KEY FACTS

⬆ **Important events in Mary I's reign**

July 1553	**Mary I becomes Queen**
January 1554	**Wyatt's rebellion – a rebellion against Mary I's proposed marriage to Philip of Spain (and perhaps against her Catholic faith)**
July 1554	**Mary I marries Philip of Spain**
January 1555	**England becomes an officially Catholic country**
February 1555	**Burning of Protestants begins**
1555	**Mary I's government starts rebuilding some ships in the navy**
June 1557	**Mary I joins Philip in his country's war against France**
January 1558	**Calais, the last English possession in France, is lost to the French**
November 1558	**Mary I dies**

➡ **Mary I's government introduced a lot of sensible changes that made the monarchy around £90 000 a year better off – a lot of money at the time. However, Mary died before the money started coming in. It was Elizabeth I who got the £90 000 a year!**

· TOP TIPS ·

When we look at evidence and draw our own conclusions, this is called interpretation. Often, as with Mary I, historians have different interpretations. When you are answering questions, try to show that you understand that different interpretations exist. A good idea is to give two possible different interpretations and then say which you think is right and why.

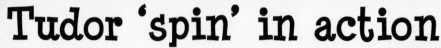

Tudor 'spin' in action

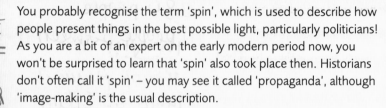

You probably recognise the term 'spin', which is used to describe how people present things in the best possible light, particularly politicians! As you are a bit of an expert on the early modern period now, you won't be surprised to learn that 'spin' also took place then. Historians don't often call it 'spin' – you may see it called 'propaganda', although 'image-making' is the usual description.

Queen Elizabeth I was a female ruler when most people thought rulers should be men – and to make matters worse had succeeded Mary I, who was probably quite unpopular. She also didn't want to get married, as was then expected of all female rulers, and therefore didn't have a clear heir, which could have made things unstable (remember the fuss about Henry VIII and a male heir) and in the latter part of her reign, she became elderly and not very attractive. She had to find some way of dealing with all this.

Although Elizabeth had many skills that helped her to be a successful ruler, she also used image-making to show herself as even more effective in the eyes of subjects and foreign powers.

Queen Elizabeth I by Nicholas Hilliard, 1574

Elizabeth and her supporters used paintings to make points about her as a ruler. The above painting was painted in 1574, by Nicholas Hilliard, it is full of <u>symbols</u> about Elizabeth. Educated people at the time would have been able to 'read' the symbols.

1　**Tudor rose:** Elizabeth might be a woman but she's a Tudor like her father Henry VIII.

2　**Pearls on dress:** pearls symbolise purity – Elizabeth is unmarried but not 'sleeping around'; she is pure, almost saint-like, and thus worthy of her country's loyalty.

3　**Pelican brooch:** The story goes that a pelican used her own blood to feed her starving young. So pelicans were used to symbolise love and self-sacrifice. Elizabeth puts her country first and is like its mother.

Elizabeth and her supporters also used books and poems to present her as a wonderful queen and life under her rule as a '<u>golden age</u>'. Spenser's poem 'The Fairy Queen' presents Elizabeth in many different (complimentary) ways: she is, for example, *Gloriana* (the fairy queen) and heir to King Arthur.

Elizabeth's court was stylish and impressive. She held special events: from 1572 onwards, a tournament – the 'Accession Day Tilt' – was held on every anniversary of her accession to the throne. Elizabeth's male courtiers dressed like knights of old and competed for her favour, like the man in the picture on the left.

George Clifford

Puzzling paintings

Here are some common symbols in Tudor paintings and what they mean (some are from this chapter, but others are not). They are muddled up. Draw lines between the columns to show how they should link together.

Symbol	Meaning
Pelican	Peace
Pearls	Faithfulness
Sieve	Purity
Dog	Purity
Olive branch	Self-sacrifice

· TOP TIPS ·

Learning to 'read' a visual source is a really important skill. Next time you go to an art gallery, look carefully at the descriptions to see if they help you 'crack' the visual clues in the pictures. Not only will it really help you as a historian, but, as you get better at reading visual clues, you will find it rather satisfying to explain what a picture stands for without having to look at the description at all.

KEY FACTS

⬆ When the English army and navy went off to meet the Spanish Armada, Elizabeth couldn't lead them because she was a woman. So she went to Tilbury, where the fleet was, and addressed them just like a general addresses their troops before a big battle. She said, 'I know I have the body but of a weak and feeble woman; but I have the heart and stomach of a king, and of a king of England too.'

Important issues in Elizabeth I's reign

➡ Religion: After all the changes of the previous years, Elizabeth tried to please as many people as possible with religion. She said that England would be Protestant, but did not encourage the strong Protestants in case they upset people. Some historians think this was a successful policy, while others feel she just ended up not pleasing anyone.

⬇ Foreign relations: As a Protestant, Elizabeth had to decide whether to get involved in wars to help Protestants abroad. She also sometimes had to protect England against rulers who thought she was heretical. For example, Philip II of Spain tried to invade England in 1588.

⬆ Being a woman: Many people did not expect Elizabeth to be a strong or successful ruler.

➡ Marriage and children: Elizabeth was not married. She may have been afraid that a husband would take away her power. Because she was unmarried, she could not produce a direct heir.

⬆ Elizabeth had a picture of Henry VIII hanging in the room where she met important visitors. She would stand in front of it in the same pose to show that, although she was a woman, she was as strong as Henry VIII.

Henry VIII

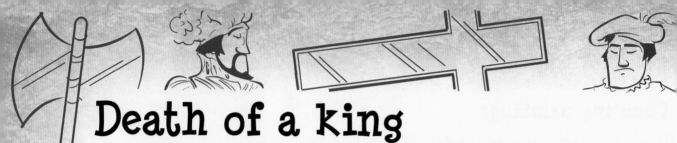

Death of a king

On a cold morning in January 1649, your family arrives in London to watch a beheading. A man is being executed for <u>treason</u>. People are whispering and talking quietly, and the air is full of expectation.

The man walks through the crowd, escorted by soldiers. He seems small and ordinary, but he is not an ordinary man. Until recently, he was King Charles I, but he was found guilty of treason and his title of king has been taken away.

The first executioner refused to execute his king, but another man is prepared to – probably for a big payout. The king kneels at the block, the executioner raises his axe and everyone holds their breath. The axe falls with a thud and the crowd groans – the king has been executed.

Charles I became king in 1625. Most people believed he was put on the throne by God and could not imagine a country without a king. But things had gone horribly wrong. A civil war had broken out. This was different to the fight between Lancastrians and Yorkists – this time the king was fighting some of his own Parliament. As the war continued, some of the King's opponents began to feel that he didn't just need to be controlled or even deposed – he needed to be executed!

Charles I's execution

How, after years of strong kings and queens like Henry VIII and Elizabeth I, had a civil war broken out?

The causes of the Civil War can be divided into 'long-term' and 'short-term'. Here are examples of what different historians believe:

Long-term causes

- People lower down in society had got more land and felt more important during the Tudor period. The Civil War was about these people wanting more political power too.

- Parliament had begun to grow in power during the Tudor period. Some MPs wanted more say in how the country was run. The Civil War can be traced back to this.

- The English Reformation was the real problem – strong Protestants (Puritans) wanted England to be more Protestant than any monarch had allowed so far. In the Civil War, Puritans were fighting to have a more Protestant country.

Short-term causes

- Charles encouraged the Archbishop of Canterbury, William Laud. Some Protestants were afraid that the Archbishop was trying to make England more Catholic, and this was not popular.

- Problems in Parliament only really started in Charles's reign – he was bad at dealing with Parliament and made things worse by trying to run the country without Parliament.

- Charles made the people pay too many taxes, which was unpopular.

- Charles was not a very skilled king. The problems became so serious because of his personal weaknesses.

Civil warring

Decide whether each of these statements is **true** or **false**.

1	Charles I was beheaded in 1459	True	☐	False	☐
2	Charles and Parliament argued about the army	True	☐	False	☐
3	A long-term cause is one where the reasons only go back a few years	True	☐	False	☐
4	Civil war broke out in 1642	True	☐	False	☐
5	Charles's Archbishop of Canterbury was unpopular because people thought he was too Protestant	True	☐	False	☐
6	Another word for a strong Protestant is a Puritan	True	☐	False	☐

KEY FACTS

'Trigger causes'

- Whether the causes are long-term, short-term or both, something also usually 'sparks off' an event. This can be called a 'trigger' cause. Many historians feel that the 'trigger' for the Civil War was an argument about the army in 1642. Charles needed an army to fight a rebellion in Ireland, but Parliament felt that he didn't deserve an army. Both king and Parliament gave orders to call an army together, and people had to decide which side to obey.

• TOP TIPS •

- When you are asked to write about causes, it useful to think about different types. For example, in this chapter we've separated them into long-term, short-term and 'trigger' causes.

- This chapter also reminds us about different interpretations. All the different causes on this page are possible interpretations (believed by some historians but not by others). So when you are writing about causes, you could talk about this.

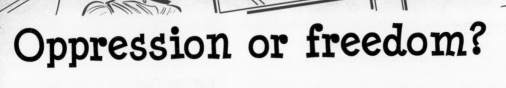

Oppression or freedom?

On a Sunday, most people like to play sport, catch up on housework or gardening, or even go to work. You may have been punished for any of these in the English Republic, when Oliver Cromwell was Lord Protector of England (1653–8). He was a general in the Civil War and ended up in charge of England. He refused the title of 'king', but was still very powerful. Cromwell and his supporters were <u>Puritans</u>. They wanted to reform the country, so that people would live holier lives and focus on God.

Some of the Puritans' actions in England have become notorious. Many people know that the <u>Protectorate</u> 'banned' Christmas. Wearing make-up and being drunk could be punished. And everyone had to respect the laws that kept Sunday a holy day.

What was life like in the Protectorate? Was it really <u>oppressive</u>?

I can think of better ways to spend the weekend

Oppressive

- Celebrating Christmas was forbidden.

- Lots of laws said what you could do on Sundays (the Christian <u>Sabbath</u>). You were not supposed to work or do unnecessary household tasks – even playing football on a Sunday could result in fines. This was because the Bible said you shouldn't work on the Sabbath.

- Women were supposed to dress modestly and weren't allowed to wear make-up. Stories tell how women's make-up was scrubbed off by keen Puritans.

- Swearing could result in a fine, and if you kept swearing you could go to prison.

Not oppressive

- People nowadays wouldn't like many of the things that happened in this period that seemed normal at the time. For example, there were few European countries where you could have got away with not going to church on a Sunday. (Even under Queen Elizabeth I, you could be fined for not going to church. If we don't realise this, Cromwell's time can seem worse than it really was.)

- Many strong Protestants would have thought that Cromwell's period actually brought freedom. For example, they would argue that people were freed from bad habits that would tempt them away from God.

- Cromwell didn't ban everything. He enjoyed listening to music and playing bowls and even had a huge party when his daughter married.

- Cromwell believed in some freedom of religion. He felt that it didn't matter which (Protestant) church Protestants went to. This means that people were allowed to be members of Protestant churches other than the Church of England. This was unusual at the time.

- Cromwell supported the Jews returning to England (the Jews had been expelled from England in 1290). Partly as a result of this, some Jewish people felt able to come to England and some who had been living secretly in England felt able to say they were Jewish.

Just punishment?

Tick **yes** or **no**, according to whether you would be punished for the following in Cromwell's England.

1 Swearing		Yes	☐	No	☐
2 Wearing make-up		Yes	☐	No	☐
3 Listening to music		Yes	☐	No	☐
4 Playing bowls		Yes	☐	No	☐
5 Being Jewish		Yes	☐	No	☐
6 Playing football on a Sunday		Yes	☐	No	☐
7 Drinking alcohol		Yes	☐	No	☐

KEY FACTS

Going to heaven?

↗ Lots of books and websites will tell you that Puritans thought they would go to heaven if they worked hard or did lots of good things. A Puritan would have been really shocked by this. Puritans actually felt that the only way to get to heaven was by having faith in Jesus as saviour of the world. The confusion comes because Puritans felt that Christians should try to live a life that was pleasing to God, partly as a 'thank you' for being saved.

Christmas is cancelled?

→ Like many other strong Protestants at the time, Cromwell believed that people had forgotten the true meaning of Christmas. Puritans felt that people weren't thinking about the birth of Jesus, their saviour. Instead, they were using Christmas as a chance to get drunk and eat too much. Strong Protestants also worried about the <u>pagan</u> things that were included in celebrations, like the use of holly. The government hoped that stopping all these celebrations would bring the focus back to the 'real meaning' of Christmas.

Other countries' laws

↙ Cromwell's England wasn't the only place to 'reform' behaviour in this way. Calvin's Geneva and John Knox's Scotland had many similar laws. For example, a man was employed to walk around Geneva to listen for the sound of a violin tuning up, because violins were often played at dances and dancing was banned. In Scotland and Geneva, Christmas was 'banned' in the same way it was under Cromwell's rule.

• TOP TIPS •

This chapter should have shown you that things often aren't as simple as they might seem. A traditional interpretation of Cromwell would say that he encouraged a very oppressive country, but you have seen that another interpretation is also possible. Try to look beyond the obvious in a topic. Ask yourself whether another possible argument exists.

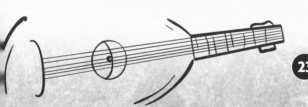

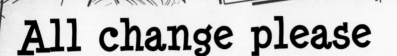

All change please

Some important people thought that it was right to depose Charles I but didn't like the Republic. They asked Charles II to be king (the Restoration). However, some of the problems that had caused the Civil War still existed. The kings felt that Parliament was power-hungry, and Parliament felt the same about them. Religion still caused problems too. People were especially worried when the Catholic James II became king – they thought he would try to make England Catholic.

There was a revolution, but it was different from the Civil War. Some important people asked William of Orange to 'save' the country. William landed with an army, but many people stayed loyal to James. It was only when the King didn't act strongly enough that the army and many politicians turned to William. James fled and Parliament made William and his wife Mary (James's Protestant daughter) joint rulers. They had to agree to conditions, including the 'Bill of Rights', before they took the throne. These mainly aimed to stop kings trying to make England Catholic, but it has been argued that they had a wider significance too.

The events of 1688 are called the 'Glorious Revolution'. Some historians say that it marked a huge change in the power of the monarchy and of Parliament. Others argue that not much changed. Read the comments below and see what you think.

Big change: yes

- For the first time, Parliament chose the monarch.

- The crown had new limits.

- Today's monarchy is 'constitutional' because laws govern what it can do. The Glorious Revolution could be said to have contributed to this with the Bill of Rights.

- Some historians argue that Parliament became so important after the Glorious Revolution that it stopped being an *event* and became an *institution* (it didn't just meet sometimes but had to meet to ensure government ran properly).

- One of William's first actions was to involve England in major European wars. It could be said that this was the start of England's attempts to become more powerful in Europe.

Big change: no

- Parliament was not always stronger after 1688: Queen Anne, for example, did much to make the monarchy stronger again.

- It could be said that Parliament only really became stronger with the accession of George I. The historian DL Farmer argues that George I and George II were happier to leave more to ministers.

- The changes were not as big as some politicians had wanted. This was because many had wanted to sort everything out quickly rather than changing the whole English system of government.

Rights or not?

Write down **right** or **not right** in the box next to each of these things that are from the Bill of Rights.

1   The monarch cannot raise taxes without Parliament's permission.

2   The monarch cannot marry a Catholic.

3   The monarch cannot have an army at all.

4   The monarch cannot stop MPs saying what they want in Parliament.

6   The monarch must retire at 70.

Glorious Revolution

Why was the revolution known as the 'Glorious Revolution'? Perhaps because it changed the way things were governed, which members of Parliament and other politicians thought was good – the end to the 'tyranny' of previous rulers. Or, perhaps because no blood was shed in England, unlike during the earlier Civil War (although blood was shed in Ireland and Scotland, as the supporters of James II fought the new rulers).

Who should rule?

The English politicians wanted to give the crown just to Mary, but William said he would not stay in England to be second in command to his wife, so the crown was offered to them both.

KEY FACTS

Bill of Rights, 1689

Some limits placed on the monarchy by the Bill of Rights were:

- the monarch cannot suspend or ignore laws

- the monarch cannot have a <u>standing army</u> without Parliament's permission

- the monarch cannot collect taxes without Parliament's permission

- the monarch cannot try to stop free speech in Parliament

- no Catholic or anyone married to a Catholic can be in line to the throne.

• TOP TIPS •

Some historians call the Glorious Revolution a **turning point**. This is a moment when things take a different direction entirely or a process of change really speeds up. You might be asked to think about whether the Glorious Revolution really was a turning point. You would need to think about what changed and what didn't. You also need to consider whether the changes were so significant that they created a turning point.

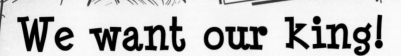

We want our king!

When James II was deposed, he had a young son – James Edward Stuart. Although he had a good claim to be king, he was Catholic. Under the Bill of Rights, he was left out of the succession. As James got older (and after Queen Anne, the last Stuart, died), some people, particularly in Scotland thought he should be king. Many Scots, particularly the Catholics, felt the Stuarts were their royal family because the Stuarts had ruled Scotland long before they ruled England.

In 1715, a rebellion tried to make James king. This was crushed in 1716, but, in 1745, another rebellion tried to make his son, Charles Edward Stuart, king. This also failed and was crushed in 1746 at the Battle of Culloden. These rebellions are known as the Jacobite Rebellions. (Jacobus is Latin for James and the Jacobites began as supporters of James II.)

James Stuart

1715 Rebellion: quick overview

Supporters of James Stuart tried to invade England (although some troops were not prepared to go any further than the English border.) In 1715, the army was defeated in England at the Battle of Preston and in Scotland, troops fought the Battle of Sheriffmuir. James landed in Scotland at the end of the year, but the English forces were too strong and he fled to France in 1716.

James Stuart was supported by:

- many Scots, especially those in the Highlands, and in particular those who didn't like the Campbells (the Campbell clan was led by a leading Scottish Whig, the Duke of Argyle and, as he supported the Hanoverians, the Campbells' enemies supported James)

- some English Tories who were angry at the Hanoverian succession

- France – although James had lots of support in France, the French king Louis XIV died in 1715, and his successor's regent was less keen on fighting England.

1745 Rebellion: quick overview

In 1745, James's son, Charles Edward Stuart, landed in Scotland with two ships given to him by the French government. He raised an army and conquered much of Scotland. He took the city of Edinburgh and beat the English at the Battle of Prestonpans. Charles's army crossed the border into England, getting as far south as Derby by December 1745. His army in Scotland won yet another battle against the English at Falkirk in January 1746. They were defeated, however, at Culloden in April 1746 (some say because the different clans began arguing about who should have the most important place in the battle). Charles escaped back to France, but his supporters were treated harshly. The government tried to break up the clans and even banned the wearing of tartan.

Charles Stuart was supported by:

- the French government: England and France were at war at this time

- many Scots, especially Catholics and those from the Highlands.

First or second placed?

Two Jacobite rebellions took place. Put a tick in the correct column to show whether the things in the first column relate to the first or second rebellion.

Battle	First rebellion	Second rebellion
Battle of Culloden	☐	☐
Battle of Preston	☐	☐
Battle of Prestonpans	☐	☐
Battle of Sheriffmuir	☐	☐
Bonnie Prince Charlie	☐	☐
Charles Edward Stuart	☐	☐
James Edward Stuart	☐	☐
The Fifteen	☐	☐
The Forty Five	☐	☐
The Old Pretender	☐	☐
The Young Pretender	☐	☐

KEY FACTS

⬆ If you try to put forward your claim to be king, but the government thinks you are not the rightful ruler, you are known as a 'pretender' (someone who makes false claims to a title). James Edward Stuart became known in history as the 'Old Pretender' and Charles Edward Stuart as the 'Young Pretender'. He is also known as 'Bonnie Prince Charlie'. (Don't get muddled – if a book talks about Bonnie Prince Charlie, the Young Pretender and Charles Edward Stuart, it's referring to the same person!)

➡ James's rebellion took place in 1715, so it often is known as the Fifteen. In the same way, Charles's rebellion often is known as the Forty Five, because it happened in 1745.

⬇ After Culloden, Charles was hunted across Scotland. A woman called Flora Macdonald is said to have saved him by disguising him as her serving maid and smuggling him past the enemy.

• TOP TIPS •

It is better to say 'many Scots supported James', rather than just saying 'the Scots supported James'. This shows you realise that not every single Scotsman was a supporter of the Pretender.

Test your knowledge 2

This assessment aims to help you to:

- practise your skills of 'reading' a source

- review the topic of Henry VIII and the break with Rome.

In this section, you will work with the source below. It is a speech made by Thomas More. More refused to swear to an act of Parliament that changed the succession to the throne because the introduction to the act said that Henry VIII was supreme head of the Church of England. More was put on trial for treason and condemned to death in 1535. This source is from his speech after the court had condemned him to death.

> 'Seeing that I see you are determined to condemn me…I will now…speak my mind plainly and freely about my condemnation and your law. For my condemnation is based upon an act of Parliament directly hateful to the laws of God and his Holy Church. The supreme government of this church…no <u>temporal</u> prince may presume by any law to take upon himself, because it rightfully belongs to the see of Rome. This is a spiritual <u>pre-eminence</u> granted by the mouth of our Saviour himself, personally present upon the earth, only to <u>St Peter and his successors</u> … No more might this realm of England refuse obedience to the see of Rome than might a child refuse obedience to his own natural father.'

Task 1
When you read a source, first make sure you understand what all the words mean. Some of the words and phrases are described on the opposite page (try to guess the meanings before looking at the suggestions), but what do you think the following phrases mean?

a   Our Saviour himself

....

b   See of Rome

....

(2 marks)

Task 2
When you read a source, you also need to make sure you know what it is saying. The following questions are designed to help you work this out.

a   Who, according to Thomas More, should be in charge of the church?

....

b   Why should this be the case?

....

(3 marks)

Task 3

Often a source doesn't say something directly, but it strongly hints at it. The following questions are about things that the source strongly hints about.

a   Why, according to Thomas More, should Henry VIII not be supreme head of the church?

....

....

b   Why should Thomas More not be condemned by this court?

....

....

(4 marks)

Task 4

Think about how the context of the source might have an impact on what was said. Thomas More had just been condemned to death when he made this speech. How might this have affected what he said?

....

....

....

....

....

(5 marks)

Task 5

Think about how the source fits into the bigger picture. How typical of people at the time do you think Thomas More was?

....

....

....

....

(5 marks)

Key phrases from the source

Pre-eminence: to be pre-eminent is to come before everyone else, to be the most important, or to have the most power.

St Peter and his successors: the popes.

Temporal: worldly. Not a member of the priesthood.

(Total 20 marks)

Let us pray

In the 1520s, a Catholic <u>monk</u>, Martin Luther, made criticisms of some of the Catholic Church's actions and beliefs. This sparked off huge changes, which led to many parts of Christian Europe rejecting the Catholic Church and setting up their own Protestant churches. If we look at the Church before the <u>Reformation</u>, we might get some clues as to why this happened. Was it because the Catholic Church was weak?

Evidence that suggests the Church was weak

- **Saints**: Protestants believed that every Christian was a saint and that praying to named saints was like worshipping false gods, which is banned by the Ten Commandments. The Dutch thinker, Erasmus, was a strong Catholic and didn't mind praying to saints, but he believed some things about saints and other religious figures were money-making 'scams'. For example, many churches and monasteries said they had a piece of the cross Jesus had died on – Erasmus said there were enough pieces of the true cross to make Noah's Ark!

- **The Renaissance Papacy**: many popes in this period do not fit with our idea of holy men. For example, Alexander VI (1492–1503) is said to have had mistresses and children, and Julius II (1503–13) was known as the 'warrior pope', because he personally led his armies into battle. Not all people then would have seen these things as wrong, but many criticised the popes for not focusing on religion.

- **Abuses**: some historians argue that abuses happened in the Church. For example, many priests and monks, who were not supposed to have sex with anyone, had mistresses. When Cardinal Cisneros tried to reform the Spanish Church, some monks went to North Africa and converted to Islam rather than give up their mistresses.

- **Unpopularity**: lots of writings criticise the Church – Chaucer's *Canterbury Tales* gives examples of immoral churchmen.

Evidence that suggests the Church was strong

- **Saints**: for many people – the rich and poor – saints were important, and people asked them to <u>intercede</u> with God. Pilgrimages to places associated with saints were popular. In England, people went on pilgrimage to the shrine of Thomas Becket in Canterbury. <u>Relics</u> of saints were popular and were thought to have special powers. This suggests people still approved of saints.

- **New religious groups**: some were new orders of monks, like the Capuchins (see 'The Church fights back?' p.34), and some were groups of <u>lay</u> people. In the Netherlands, the 'Brethren of the Common Life' tried to focus on building personal relationships with God.

- **Popes**: the Renaissance Papacy was not all bad. Julius II tried to sack important bishops thought to have bought their positions. He also commissioned Michelangelo to paint the Sistine Chapel ceiling – one of the most famous religious art works of all time. Popes glorified themselves by paying for such art, but they glorified God too, because many paintings were about religious topics.

- **Abuse**: some historians argue that abuses weren't as widespread as thought and that people probably didn't mind them as much as they might today.

- **Monasteries**: monasteries played a really important part in many people's lives – they could provide shelter for travellers, hospitals and schools. Many people supported monasteries.

- **Unpopularity**: a lot of people gave money to the Church, which suggests it wasn't completely unpopular. Remember that many writings against the Church had a purpose: Chaucer wanted to entertain, so he might have exaggerated for effect – like satirical shows on TV today. Some of Chaucer's Church characters were in fact moral, not immoral.

Praying people

All the people described below are mentioned in this chapter. Write the correct name next to each description.

1 A pope from a notorious Italian family called the Borgias. He was supposed to have had mistresses and children.

2 A pope who led his troops into battle but was also a patron of the arts.

3 A strong Catholic <u>theologian</u> who criticised some aspects of the Catholic Church (such as abuses to do with relics).

4 Writer of the *Canterbury Tales*.

KEY FACTS

Who was who in the Medieval Catholic Church?

⬆ **Priests:** looked after people's spiritual well-being and were important in helping people to live as Christians. Without a priest, for instance, people couldn't be baptised or married, and only a priest could take <u>mass</u>. Everyone in Europe was part of a parish, which covered a village or part of a town. Some parish priests did not live in their parishes, leaving all their work to a badly paid assistant.

➡ **Bishops:** were Church leaders who had an area that they were responsible for called a <u>diocese</u> (sometimes called a see or a bishopric), made up of lots of parishes. Bishops sometimes had a big role in politics as well as religion.

⬇ **Pope:** head of the Catholic Church on earth. Lived in Rome, in the Vatican.

⬆ **Monks and nuns:** these were members of religious orders who had made a promise to live together in a community, praying and sometimes helping the poor. Monks often lived in *monasteries* (sometimes called abbeys or priories) but also worked in the local community.

⬅ Getting a job in the Church was a good way for an ordinary person to become important. Many powerful bishops came from quite humble backgrounds.

• TOP TIPS •

When looking at this period, it is important not to judge it from our own values. For example, you might disapprove of a priest having a mistress, but some historians point out that many people accepted this at the time.

A monk changes Europe

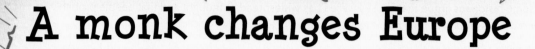

Martin Luther was a German from an ordinary family. Not many people could afford to send their children to school, but Luther's father, a miner, managed to make some money and paid for him to go to school. His parents hoped he would become a lawyer. His teacher, like every teacher at the time, beat his students if they got things wrong. However, he started classes by bowing to his students, because he said they would all become important people.

One day, Luther was caught in a thunderstorm. He was so terrified that he vowed to St Anne that he would become a monk if he was saved from the storm. He did become a monk (to his father's dismay) and began to study theology. Eventually, he became a professor at the University of Wittenberg, Germany.

Luther became worried about some of the doctrine and practices of the Church. He felt that the Church put too much emphasis on doing things to get to Heaven. Luther believed that you couldn't make yourself good enough to go to Heaven, that only faith and trust in Jesus would save you.

Luther wrote his ideas in Latin and nailed them to the door of the University Church in Wittenberg, so other theologians would talk about the ideas. A printer took Luther's ideas, translated them into German and printed them. They became a 'bestseller' among the ordinary people. This angered the Catholic Church, which tried to make Luther 'take back' his ideas, but he refused.

Luther got into lots of trouble – the Church was angry with him and the German <u>Diet</u> declared him an outlaw. (This meant that anyone who killed him wouldn't be punished). Luther went into hiding, but he stuck by his ideas. Other people supported him, and, over time, Luther got more supporters and founded a new Church – the Protestant Church.

Possible causes of the German Reformation

- Personality: Luther was not the sort to back down if he thought he was right. He had a really strong temper and was very determined.

- Politics: the local ruler of Luther's area, the <u>Elector</u> of Saxony, supported Luther because he agreed with his ideas. The man in overall charge of the Holy Roman Empire was the Emperor Charles V. He wanted to stop Luther, but the Elector of Saxony wanted to show that Charles V didn't have any right to tell his subjects what to do. If rulers like the Elector of Saxony hadn't supported Luther, he would have been arrested, his followers burnt for heresy and the Reformation probably wouldn't have happened. Also, many ordinary Germans liked the idea of a German monk attacking a church ruled by a foreign pope.

- Church: some people supported Luther because they liked his ideas about how to get to heaven. Others thought the Catholic Church was corrupt and liked the idea of joining a new Church, which they thought might be less corrupt.

Veni Sancte Spiritus

Lutheran lessons!

1 What did Luther's father do for a living?

2 What was the Schmalkaldic League?

3 What was a Diet?

4 Who ruled the area in which Luther lived?

5 Who was the man in overall charge of the Holy Roman Empire?

6 Who is the head of the Catholic Church on earth?

7 Give the name of a city that became 'Lutheran'.

8 What do you think 'Lutheran' means?

KEY FACTS

⬆ **Key events**

1517	Luther nails his ideas, the '95 Theses', on a church door in Wittenberg.
1517–19	Luther is questioned by members of the Church, who try to persuade him to change his mind.
1520–21	Luther is excommunicated (thrown out of the Church) and declared an outlaw.
1520s–30s	Many cities in Germany, such as Nuremberg, decide to accept Luther's ideas for their churches. Many German princes and dukes decide to make their churches 'Lutheran'.
1531	The Protestant rulers set up the 'Schmalkaldic League', which was like a club with an army. They wanted to protect themselves from attack by the Catholic rulers.
1547	The Battle of Mühlberg. Charles V and the Catholic princes fight the Protestant princes. The Catholic army wins, but the Catholic rulers are worried that Charles's victory will make him too powerful so…
1555	The Diet meets at the city of Augsburg and decides that each ruler can decide whether to make their own area Catholic or Lutheran.

➡ Why are Protestants called 'Protestants'? Many people think it was because they 'protested' (complained) about the Catholic Church. Actually, it was because in 1529, after a Diet (at Speyer), some supporters of Luther protested that the Diet was making laws that were too hard on them.

⬇ Luther wasn't the only theologian to challenge the Catholic Church at this time – other reformers included Zwingli in Zurich and, very importantly, Calvin in Geneva. The reformers' ideas spread across Europe and beyond.

• TOP TIPS •

If you are writing about causes, it is a good idea to show how these causes might affect each other. For example, you might think that Luther's personality wouldn't have been so important if it hadn't been for the politics in the Empire. By saying this, you would be showing that you understand that causes are linked together.

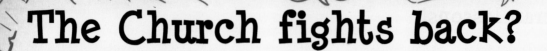

The Church fights back?

In the 16th century, the Catholic Church underwent many reforms.

Some historians think this was a response to <u>Protestantism</u>. They believe the Catholic Church wanted to protect itself against the Protestant Church. Many reforms took place after Luther's ideas started spreading ,or focused on things that Luther had challenged. Historians describe these reforms as the 'Counter-Reformation' (Reformation against the Protestants).

Other historians say that many reforms happened before Luther's ideas spread. They believe that the 1520s are probably too early for examples of the Catholics fighting the Protestants, because the Catholic Church still saw Luther as a problem for just parts of Germany – not the whole Church. Even things that had happened later than 1520 might still just have been motivated by a desire for reform for its own sake.The Catholic Church reformed itself because reforms were needed and would have done it without the Protestants. Historians who believe this call the reforms the 'Catholic Reformation'.

Council of Trent

The Council of Trent was a meeting of important churchmen; they met regularly between 1545 and 1563. Its main topics were:

I do hope the washing machine is fixed soon!

- doctrine: it restated Catholic beliefs clearly and focused on the beliefs Luther challenged

- <u>discipline</u>: it set new standards for priests and bishops – e.g. a bishop had to visit every parish in his see at least once every two years.

Jesuits

The Jesuits were a <u>religious order</u> founded by the Spanish ex-soldier, Ignatius Loyola, in 1540. They were one of the most important groups in the Catholic Reformation. Loyola and his early supporters wanted to go to the <u>Holy Land</u> to spread Christianity, but the Pope used them to support Catholics in their faith and to win Protestants back to <u>Roman Catholicism</u>. In time, the Jesuits also went abroad to convert people from other faiths to Christianity.

Other new orders

Many other Catholic religious orders were set up all over Europe, which suggests a new excitement in the Catholic Church and a real desire for people to get involved in the Catholic faith.

- In 1520, in the south of Italy, four friends formed a group so they could spend some time living as <u>hermits</u> and some time helping the poor. In 1528, the Pope allowed them to form the Capuchin order.

- In Spain in 1562, Teresa of Ávila set up the '<u>Discalced</u> Carmelites'. She had been a Carmelite nun but felt the nuns lived in luxury, so she started her own branch of the order. Teresa also had many personal religious experiences such as visions of God's love.

Inquisitions

Inquisitions checked that Catholics had the right beliefs. The Spanish Inquisition was started in 1478 (before Luther was born). It was first designed to deal with Jews who converted to Catholicism (lots of prejudice against the Jews existed, and some people suspected that converts had not 'really' converted). The Spanish Inquisition was used later to stamp out other <u>heresies</u>, like Protestantism. Other inquisitions were set up or revived in the 16th century, such as the Papal Inquisition in 1542.

Rulers

Many rulers worked hard to protect and encourage Catholic beliefs in their countries. Philip II, King of Spain between 1556 and 1598, sometimes argued with the papacy. He was, however, a strong supporter of Catholicism in his own lands and sometimes fought other non-Catholic rulers, such as Elizabeth I.

Popes

Popes in this period were very different from the 'Renaissance Papacy'.

- **Adrian VI (1522–23)**: when he became pope, he said he wanted to reform the Church, starting with the papacy. He said that the 'entire world [was] longing for such a Reformation'. However, he died before he could do very much.

- **Paul IV (1555–59):** he worked hard to protect Catholic beliefs. For instance, he set up the Index in 1559. This was a list of heretical books that Catholics should not read.

- **Pius V (1566–72)**: he worked hard to 'clean up' Rome to make it less immoral. He also was known for personal holiness. Pius was declared a saint after his death.

Mistaken statements

Correct the mistakes in these sentences.

1 Pope Pius V wanted to reform the Catholic Church but died (in 1523) before he could really do anything.

2 The Council of Trent started meeting in 1545. This was before Martin Luther nailed his 95 theses to the door.

3 An inquisition had been set up in Germany in 1478 to deal with Jewish people who had converted to Christianity.

4 A hermit is a person who lives with lots of other people so that they can party.

5 The original Jesuits wanted to go to Germany to convert Protestants.

· TOP TIPS ·

Sometimes things as simple as dates can help us answer historical problems. If something was set up before Luther's ideas began spreading (in the 1520s onwards), it couldn't have been set up just to attack Protestantism (although remember that it doesn't mean everything after 1520 was motivated by an attack on Protestant ideas).

Test your knowledge 3

This assessment aims to help you to:

- practise your source work further

- develop your understanding of the Lutheran Reformation.

In 1521, Martin Luther was called before the German Diet. He was interrogated by theologians and asked to recant his ideas (say that they were wrong). The people at the Diet included Charles, the young Holy Roman Emperor. He was ruler of modern-day Germany, Austria, the Netherlands and Spain. Below is Luther's reply to the Diet.

'Since then Your Majesty and your lordships desire a simple reply, I will answer without horns and without teeth. Unless I am convicted by scripture and plain reason (I do not accept the authority of popes and councils...) my conscience is captive to the Word of God. I cannot and I will not recant anything, for to go against conscience is neither right nor safe. God help me. Amen'

Without horns and without teeth: Plainly

You are going to use this source to find out more about the character of Martin Luther. You will also think about how Luther's character might have had an effect on the Reformation.

Task 1
Read through the source. What does it tell us about Luther?

(Tip: there's not just one answer here. Read the source and think about what sort of person might say things like this. I've suggested some possible answers in the answer section, but you might think of different ones.)

....

....

....

....

....

....

....

(5 marks)

Task 2

Now think about what the source means for your understanding of the Reformation. How does what you learnt about Luther in this source help you understand why the Reformation was successful in Germany?

....

....

....

....

....

....

....

(5 marks)

Task 3

Now fit this in with the bigger picture. Stick with the question, 'Why was the Reformation successful in Germany?' What can you add from what you know already? Do you know anything more about Luther as a person? Does this fit with what you know from the source or does it contradict it? What about other reasons? Was Luther's character the only reason the Reformation did well in Germany?

....

....

....

....

....

....

....

(5 marks)

(Total 15 marks)

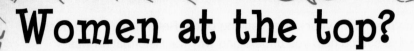

Women at the top?

In 1603, Elizabeth I died without an heir. Her first cousin three times removed, James, therefore became ruler of England after her death. He became King James I of England, but he was already a king – King James VI of Scotland. When James became King of England, the two countries – England and Scotland – had the same ruler. However it was not until 1707 that an act of Parliament formally brought the two countries together.

What about Scotland before 1603? It's easy to forget that before 1603 Scotland had its own king and was completely independent (although that didn't stop the English and French kings trying to interfere!). The history of Scotland 1488–1603 is one of huge changes and big events – the death of kings, the rule of women and the changing of religion from Catholic to Protestant.

Women in power

We often think that only men ruled in this period, but three of the Scottish rulers were women.

- **Margaret Tudor:** widow of James IV of Scotland and mother of James V. Henry VII's daughter and Henry VIII's sister. <u>Regent</u> for her son, James V, for a time.

- **Mary of Guise:** mother of Mary Stuart and widow of James V. Regent of Scotland 1554–60. A very strong woman. Some historians think she governed Scotland very cleverly; while others believe she made the Scots too resentful of the French.

- **Mary Stuart (Mary, Queen of Scots):** Queen of Scotland from 1542 to 1567, but she was sent to France in 1548 to marry Francis, the <u>Dauphin</u>. He became King of France in 1559. If he had lived, their heir might have inherited the crowns of Scotland and France and these countries might have been joined together, but he died in 1560 and Mary returned to Scotland, where her troubles really began. Her poor control of government and bad luck with men meant she was forced to abdicate. She fled to England, but her cousin, Elizabeth, imprisoned her. Mary was imprisoned for almost 20 years. She was a Catholic, so some Catholics of Elizabeth's enemies tried to make her queen instead of Elizabeth. In the end, evidence of Mary's direct involvement in a plot was discovered, and she was executed.

The Auld Alliance

Scotland and France traditionally allied with each other against England in the 'Auld Alliance'. This was bad news for England, because Scotland and France could plan joint attacks. The alliance could be good for Scotland, because the French helped protect them against England, but also bad because France could try to get too much power in Scotland.

SUGAR

Veni Sancte Spiritus

Sussed your Scots?

Under each clue, write down the name of the Scottish ruler being described.

Mother of Mary Queen of Scots	Killed in battle	Became King of England in 1603	Executed by Elizabeth I	Grandson of Henry VII

KEY FACTS

⬆ **James IV:** came to throne in 1488 after James III died. Supported Perkin Warbeck against Henry VII for a while, but then made peace with Henry and married his daughter Margaret. This brought peace between the two countries for a while, but when Henry VIII became king, the two countries fought again. James IV was killed at the Battle of Flodden in 1513.

➡ **James V:** became king after his father, but he was only a boy. His regents were his mother Margaret, who supported the English, then a cousin, the Duke of Albany, who opposed England, and then Margaret again. When James became an adult, he married a French princess; when she died, he married a French noblewoman, Mary of Guise. Henry VIII did not like James's support of the French and invaded Scotland. The Scots were defeated at the battle of Solway Moss (1542), and James died days after – perhaps from the shock of losing the battle.

⬇ **Mary Stuart:** James V's daughter. She was only one week old when her father died and she became queen, but regents ruled on her behalf until 1561. These included her mother, Mary of Guise. When Mary of Guise died, in 1560, some Scottish Protestants, who were already very important, took control of the government and made Scotland Protestant. When Mary Stuart came home, she found she had very little power, and she made matters worse by having affairs. She was even suspected of being involved in a plot to murder one of her husbands. She had to <u>abdicate</u> in 1567, and she ran away to England, where she was kept prisoner by Elizabeth I and eventually was executed for treason.

⬆ **James VI:** when Mary abdicated, her young son James became James VI. At first, he was controlled by the Scottish Protestants, but when he came of age he made himself much more powerful. For example, he made sure he had some power over the Church. Scotland was quite a poor country, however, so when James was made King of England, he probably went to England quite happily, hoping it would be a richer country!

• TOP TIPS •

When you write about the Tudor period, make sure you show the reader that you know England and Scotland were two separate countries. For example, you should talk about 'England' or 'Scotland' and not 'Britain'. If you are asked to write about England's 'foreign policy' (its relations with foreign countries), make sure you include Scotland as one of the foreign countries.

The origins of tensions?

The tensions in Northern Ireland between the Catholics and Protestants are often in the news. Many Protestants want Northern Ireland to remain part of the United Kingdom and many Catholics want it to become part of the Republic of Ireland, Eire, instead. Some people have felt so strongly about this, that they have been prepared to fight to get want they want.

These tensions are not new. Many historians argue that the they can be traced at least to the Tudor period. At the start of this period, English kings were 'Lords of Ireland', and Ireland was ruled by a 'Lord Deputy', who represented the English king in Ireland. English kings controlled only a tiny bit of Ireland directly, however, and this was called 'The Pale', which included Dublin and the land around it.

Some other parts of Ireland were ruled by 'Anglo-Irish lords' from old Norman families. They went to Ireland when Henry II conquered parts of Ireland, but by the Tudor period, they saw things in an 'Irish' way. They sometimes supported the English kings, but only when it suited them, and English kings didn't have the time or power to force them. In other parts of Ireland, such as the far north and south, the English king's power didn't exist at all. The nobles were native Irish – 'Gaelic lords' – and had no historical loyalty to the English crown.

> Your behaviour beyond the pale

Between 1485 and 1750, things changed. English rulers tried to extend English power over Ireland. The Reformation caused problems, because English rulers tried to impose Protestantism on Ireland. There were revolts, rebellions and massacres. By the end of this period, the seeds for modern difficulties in Ireland had already been sown.

Different types of Irish

*   **Gaelic Irish or 'Old Irish':** much of Ireland was ruled by native, Gaelic Irish people at the start of the period. After the Reformation, they mostly stayed Catholic. Gaelic Irish often had few rights.

*   **Anglo-Irish or 'Old English':** people who moved to Ireland with the Norman invaders. They had some loyalty to the English, especially at the start, but saw themselves at least as much Irish as English. They mainly stayed Catholic, and they increasingly began to work more closely with the Old Irish.

*   **Protestant Settlers or 'New English':** brought in by the later Tudors and Stuarts to take over land and make Ireland more loyal to England and more Protestant.

Why did the English want more power in Ireland?

This question has many answers. In part, rulers wanted more power for the sake of it, but they were also afraid that their enemies might use Ireland as a 'launching pad' for an invasion. This was especially true after the Reformation, when the English government was scared of the threat from Catholic countries like Spain.

Beyond the pale

The saying 'beyond the pale' means unacceptable. The Pale was the part of Ireland controlled directly by the English. The English people felt that the Pale was where civilised people lived and that the area outside the Pale was full of uncivilised 'barbarians' who did not act acceptably. This is where the saying comes from.

Veni Sancte Spiritus

Grasped your Gaelic?

1 Who were the following in Ireland?

   a) Old Irish ....

   b) Old English ....

   c) New English ....

2 What job did the Earl of Kildare have under Henry VIII?

....

3 What were plantations?

....

4 What happened at Drogheda?

....

• TOP TIPS •

This topic is a great chance for you to show that you understand how events in the past have an impact on events today. You might be asked to write about how successful rulers were in Ireland 1485–1750. If so, you would mainly look at their success within this period, but you could also write a paragraph discussing whether their mistakes were so serious that their consequences are still with us today.

KEY FACTS

⬆ **Henry VII's reign (1485–1509):** Henry's main worry was that the Anglo-Irish would support pretenders. The Earl of Kildare was suspended as Lord Deputy of Ireland because of his attitude to Simnel and Warbeck. Henry made Sir Edward Poynings, an Englishman, Lord Deputy to try to increase royal power in Ireland. He did this but it was too expensive to keep him there, and Kildare was given his job back.

➡ **Henry VIII's reign (1509–47):** Henry made himself Supreme Head of the Church in Ireland as well as England. Henry also made himself King of all Ireland. Gaelic Irish lords became nobles like the English nobles.

⬇ **Edward VI's and Mary I's reigns (1547–58):** Edward tried to introduce Protestant ideas, but then Mary's government did a good job of bringing back Catholic ideas. Some English were sent over as colonists to try to make Ireland more loyal.

⬆ **Elizabeth I's reign (1558–1603):** Ireland became more and more Catholic, as many Jesuit priests went to Ireland. This caused a lot of tension, even between the Anglo-Irish and the government. There were two rebellions: one in 1569 and one in 1598. The second was especially difficult for the English to put down. The English government had two ways of trying to get more power in Ireland. One was to use force, and the other was a policy of <u>plantation</u>. This was very unpopular.

⬅ **Early Stuarts and Commonwealth (1603–88):** The unpopular policy of plantation continued and, as a result, the Old English became less and less loyal to the English government. A huge rebellion started in 1641, and, in the early 1650s, Oliver Cromwell's troops came to Ireland to punish the rebels, many of whom were massacred at the town of Drogheda.

➡ **After the Glorious Revolution (1688–1750):** because James II was a Catholic, he went to Ireland after he was deposed in England; however, William of Orange defeated him at the Battle of the Boyne. William, and his daughter Anne, passed laws called the 'penal laws', which said that Protestants should have the power in Ireland.

One country?

Have you wondered why the Eurovision Song Contest has one entrant for the whole United Kingdom but Ireland, Scotland, Wales and England have their own teams in the football World Cup?

In 1485, Scotland was separate from England. Wales and Ireland were under some English control but were not fully part of the kingdom. 'On paper', the four kingdoms were <u>united</u> by 1750, but in many ways they were not united at all. Some kingdoms kept aspects of their own systems and cultures, and many Welsh, Scots and Irish resented the English rulers.

British Isles in 1485

- **England:** ruled by the King of England, although some parts of England had their own laws. Ely, for example, had quite a lot of <u>independence</u>, and nobles in the Scottish and Welsh borders (the 'Marches') were allowed more independence because they were at risk of invasion from Welsh rebels and Scottish armies.

- **Scotland:** ruled by the King of Scotland. <u>Independent</u> from England. Often <u>allied</u> with France against England.

- **Wales:** a <u>principality</u> ruled by the Prince of Wales (eldest son of the English king). Wales didn't follow the English laws and had its own culture and language. Many Welsh disliked the English, and the English kings' laws often weren't obeyed.

- **Ireland:** a small part of Ireland around Dublin, the Pale, was directly under the English kings' control. Technically, the kings of England were lords of Ireland, but in many places English control was weak. In the south, around the Pale, most nobles had come to Ireland after the Norman Conquest. They were Anglo-Irish lords and were loyal to the English kings. Further north and in some places in the South, the nobles were from older families – the Gaelic chieftains – and were not loyal to the English kings.

British Isles in 1750

- **England:** ruled by the King of England (although Parliament had more influence than before). The same law was in place throughout England.

- **Scotland:** completely under English control – the English kings were also kings of Scotland. The Scots sent members of Parliament to Westminster rather than having their own Parliament, but they kept their own church system and law courts. Although the Jacobite rebellion had been put down, many Scots resented the English.

- **Wales:** much more clearly under English control. Although it had the same laws as England, Wales remained a principality. English language and customs were more fashionable, but the Welsh language and culture was still strong.

- **Ireland:** the English kings were also kings of Ireland, and all English laws were technically also Irish laws. Many Protestant settlers were sent to the north of Ireland to make it more loyal (policy of plantations), but much tension existed between the English and Irish, and between the Protestant Irish and Catholic Irish.

Veni Sancte Spiritus

Union links

Draw a line to link each statement with its correct date.

Act of Union between Wales and England

Act of Union between Scotland and England

English kings start calling themselves kings of Ireland

James VI of Scotland becomes King James I of England

Henry Tudor (a Welsh noble) becomes King of England.

1603

1541   **1485**

1536

1707

KEY FACTS

1536 Welsh Act of Union. Wales has its first members of Parliament, and English laws are brought to Wales. This is followed by another act in 1543.

1536 Places within England that had special freedoms ('liberties'), such as Ely, are brought fully under the government's control.

1541 Henry VIII takes the title 'King of Ireland'.

1603 King James VI of Scotland becomes James I of England. After this, England and Scotland have the same king.

1707 Act of Union between England and Scotland.

Prince of Wales

⬆ Technically, Wales is a principality. This means that it is ruled by a prince. Traditionally the Prince of Wales is the eldest son of the English monarch.

• TOP TIPS •

By looking at what changed and what stayed the same, you will be in a better position to assess how far, or to what extent, something changed. If you are asked how far something changed, you should make a clear judgement. For example, if you are asked how far the United Kingdom really was united by 1750, you might say 'it was very united' or 'not united at all'.

Towards empire?

At one point, like many European countries, Britain ruled many places around the world. Under Queen Victoria (1837–1901), the British <u>Empire</u> was huge. During the period covered in this book, the British Empire was just starting to develop.

Precious fish?

Henry VII supported John Cabot in his attempt to find a new route to Asia, where a lot of money could be made in precious spices. In 1497, John landed on a new shore, but it wasn't Asia. Instead he had 'discovered' what is now known as Newfoundland in Canada. Instead of being rich in spices, it was rich in fish!

American Indians

The natives in North America are sometimes called Indians, although a better term is Native Americans. They often welcomed and supported settlers, but there was also violence and misunderstanding on both sides. Native Americans and settlers were both known to attack each other.

The slave trade

At first, almost all workers in British colonies were British settlers, but the work soon needed lots more people. The British started using the 'triangular' slave trade. In the first part of the triangle, ships sailed from America to Britain, full of things like tobacco and sugar, which were sold in Britain. The ships then sailed to Africa, full of things the African slave traders wanted, and the slave traders sold African slaves to the British. These slaves were taken, in terrible conditions, mainly to the West Indies. By 1724, 75% of the population of Barbados were black slaves.

Some motives for overseas expansion and colonisation

- **Trade**: many explorers were looking for new sources of trade, so they or their patrons could make money. For example, people in Barbados started making money from tobacco and then sugar.

- **Prestige**: explorers and their patrons wanted fame and fortune. Also countries with an empire looked good.

- **New opportunities**: many people saw the chance to start a new life and to make money.

- **Religious freedom**: some people went to America to found colonies where they could have more religious freedom than in Europe. In 1620, the Pilgrim Fathers sailed from Plymouth in their ship, the Mayflower, and set up a colony in New England in North America.

Veni Sancte Spiritus

Empire events

Choose the correct date for when each event took place; you do not need to use every date.

1627	1497	1524
1597	1436	1690
1655	1664	1350
1708	1620	1497

1 First colony in Barbados
2 John Cabot sails from Bristol and 'discovers' Newfoundland
3 Mayflower sets sail from Plymouth
4 New Amsterdam captured
5 Jamaica captured
6 Calcutta set up

KEY FACTS

North America

This was the main area in which Britain expanded during the period covered by this book.

⬆ The first places 'discovered' were in what we call Canada. By 1750, Britain had colonies in much of this part of America, including Hudson Bay and Nova Scotia.

➡ Britain also had many colonies along the east coast of America. Sir Walter Raleigh was the first person to try to set up a colony there – in Roanoke, Virginia, in 1584. This settlement failed, but over the years, people became more successful. The first colony that survived was started in Jamestown, Virginia in 1607. Many more colonies were set up at this time. Britain also gained some colonies from other foreign powers: in 1664, the English captured the Dutch colony of New Netherlands, which included the city of New Amsterdam (which was renamed New York).

⬇ Britain also gained colonies in the West Indies in the Caribbean: Barbados was first settled in 1627, and the English captured Jamaica from the Spanish in 1655.

India

⬆ Britain was expanding into India by the end of the period covered in this book. In 1600, the East India Company was set up to trade with countries in Asia, but it soon became interested in setting up <u>trading stations</u> in India. The company was mainly interested in making money from trade, but it was good for them to control some of the land to protect their trade. In 1640, the English were given Madras by the local rulers, and they founded the city of Calcutta in 1690. The company was also prepared to fight locals; moreover, by the end of the period, the British Empire in India wasn't as big as it would later become.

· TOP TIPS ·

Remember that people lived in these places before the Europeans turned up. It's not a good idea, for example, to write that John Cabot discovered Newfoundland, because the people who lived there already knew about it. If you are going to use this word, put it in quotation marks – John Cabot 'discovered' Newfoundland.

Test your knowledge 4

This assessment aims to help you to:

- produce a piece of extended writing

- think through changes in government in the British Isles during the period 1485–1750.

In this section, you are going to think about the question, 'Had the monarchy become weaker by 1750?' Many of the chapters in this section will be helpful, but you will also find earlier chapters of the book useful, such as the chapter 'All change!'.

Task 1
Think of some ways in which the monarchy had become weaker by 1750. Make a list below.

....

....

....

....

....

....

....

....

....

(10 marks)

Task 2
Now think of the other side of the argument. Are there arguments against the things you have said above? Are there any other arguments?

....

....

....

....

....

....

....

....

....

(10 marks)

Task 3

What is your conclusion? Which is the most convincing? Do you think that, overall, the monarchy had become weaker by 1750?

....

....

....

....

....

....

....

....

....

....

(15 marks)

(Total 25 marks)

Curtain up!

What do you like to do for entertainment? Do you enjoy the cinema, music or theatre? Do you like watching sport or losing yourself in a good novel? If you lived in London during the 1590s, you would probably have loved going to see a new play, perhaps by the actor and writer William Shakespeare. As many as 21 000 Londoners probably went to the theatre at least once a week – about one in eight Londoners at the time!

Going to the theatre in the late Elizabethan period wasn't like going to the theatre today. For a start, theatres were partly open air, just like the reconstruction of Shakespeare's Globe Theatre in London. If you had bought cheap tickets, you would be a 'groundling' and would stand in front of the stage – if it rained, you got wet! The plays would have taken place during the day because there was no lighting. There was also not much scenery, and most plays would have been performed in modern dress. The audiences were much less 'polite' than today – they would often shout to the characters in the play and would sometimes try to get involved.

The threatre wasn't the only place for entertainment in 1590. You could (especially if you were a man) have gone to the 'cockpits', where trained cockerels fought each other, with people watching and betting on the result...or you could have gone to a nearby tavern (pub). You could even go to a brothel. Theatres were near all these places, so theatres weren't for only very 'cultured' people – just another source of entertainment for everyone.

Ups and downs of the Globe Theatre

The first Elizabethan playhouse was called the Theatre and was built in 1576. Others included the Rose, Curtain, Swan and Globe (built in 1599). The first Globe Theatre had to be pulled down and rebuilt on the south bank of the Thames because its owners hadn't sorted out the lease properly. In 1612, it burnt down during a play after a gun, fired as part of the play, set light to the thatched roof. It was rebuilt again, but the Puritans pulled it down in 1644.

Women in theatre

Women didn't act on the stage until well after Shakespeare's time; instead, women's parts were taken by boys whose voices hadn't broken. Whole companies were formed of boy actors, who were often choirboys, like the Children of the Chapel Royal. Boys' companies started to perform in public in the 1570s and were popular until the early 17th century. Women started to act in plays from the middle of the 17th century, but it was a while before there were enough actresses to go round. This meant that the use of boys died out gradually – not all at once.

Actors and vagrants

Actors in the middle ages were often 'travelling players', but by Elizabeth I's reign, travelling players could be convicted for vagrancy. The only solution was to form 'troupes' under important men, so companies, such the Lord Chamberlain's Men, were formed. Companies like this started using the new theatres or 'playhouses'.

The royal court

In the early part of this book's period, writers produced some plays for the royal court, which were rather like short morality plays. During the Elizabethan period, the acting companies often went to the court with their plays. Many plays were written especially for court celebrations. Shakespeare's *Twelfth Night* is thought to have been written for a twelfth-night feast at court. In the Jacobean period, 'masques' were very popular at court. These were like short plays, with music and very ambitious scenery (often designed by famous architects like Inigo Jones).

Theatrical antics

Circle the correct answer.

1 Which of these things did not happen to the Globe theatre?

| a fire | being closed down by the Puritans |

| having to move because the lease went wrong |

| getting a roof which sheltered audiences from the rain |

2 Which of these is not a play by Shakespeare?

| A Midsummer Night's Dream | The Alchemist |

| Twelfth Night | Hamlet |

3 Boys took women's roles until at least the mid-17th century.

| True | False |

• TOP TIPS •

If you are talking about changes over time, make sure you actually give examples of key changes from across the period. Be especially careful to talk about how things were at the start and how they were at the end.

KEY FACTS

Quick tour of theatre in this period

⬆ **Mystery and morality:** at the start of this book's period, ordinary people would have mainly watched mystery plays and morality plays. Mystery plays acted out Bible stories, while in morality plays, such as *Everyman* (1490), actors symbolised good and bad characteristics such as greed or kindness. Usually these plays were acted in the open air. They could be very dramatic and tried hard to be realistic. For example, animal blood was used if someone was stabbed in a play.

⬆ **Age of Shakespeare:** during the later years of the reigns of Elizabeth I and James I, the most famous playwright was William Shakespeare. He wrote many plays, including *Macbeth, Hamlet, Romeo and Juliet* and *A Midsummer Night's Dream*. Many other people were also writing plays at this time, such as Christopher Marlowe (who died young in mysterious circumstances) and Ben Jonson. Marlowe's plays include *Dr Faustus*, which is about a man who sells his soul to the devil, and Ben Jonson's include *The Alchemist*, a comedy about a group of con men.

⬆ **Blood and guts:** in the early Stuart period, tragedies became very bloodthirsty. Not only did many characters die horribly, but they'd normally have really horrible things happen to them or do really horrible things themselves (or both). John Webster's plays, *The White Devil* and *The Duchess of Malfi*, are good examples.

➡ **Restoration drama:** Charles II reopened the playhouses (the Puritans had closed them). Theatres were now indoors, like some Jacobean theatres, rather than outdoors, like the Globe (the Theatre Royal, Drury Lane, comes from this period). The most famous plays from this period are comedies, written by people like William Congreve (1678–1707). In this period, going to the theatre became more of a hobby for richer people, whereas in Shakespeare's time, all types of people had enjoyed the theatre.

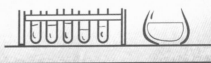

An ideal home?

Everyone has a different ideal home. People are often influenced by what is fashionable. Old Victorian terraced houses used to be really unpopular, and many were demolished to make 'modern' shopping centres. Now, lots of people want to live in the terraces, so they cost a lot of money. Tastes also changed during the period from 1485 to 1750.

Changing safety

At the start of the Tudor period, many nobles lived in <u>fortified</u> or semi-fortified houses, like Oxburgh Hall in Norfolk, which was started in 1482. This was partly because the style was fashionable, and partly because there was always a danger of attack during the Wars of the Roses, so people felt safer in buildings surrounded by moats.

Oxburgh Hall

As the country became safer, houses didn't need so much protection. Hardwick Hall, for example, was built in the 1590s by Bess of Hardwick, a friend of Elizabeth I. Locals used to say, 'Hardwick Hall, more glass than wall', because of the large number of windows.

Changing fashions

Over this book's period, fashions also changed. Ideas from the <u>Renaissance</u> were taken up: Hampton Court Palace (begun in the 1510s), for example, has pictures of Roman emperors in its courtyards. Hardwick Hall was built in a very Renaissance style. Architecture inspired by <u>classical</u> designs became even more popular during the Stuart period, as the picture of the Queen's House at Greenwich, with its classical columns, shows. This was built between 1616 and 1635 and was designed by Inigo Jones.

Harwick Hall

By the time of the Great Fire of London (1666), tastes had changed again. Much of London was rebuilt in the new <u>baroque</u> style. St Paul's Cathedral is a wonderful example.

Queen's House

Town houses

The sort of houses seen in towns also changed. Tudor townhouses from Alcester, near Stratford-upon-Avon, had <u>exposed timbers</u>, which were really fashionable. Compare these with the house in Alton, Hampshire (25 Lenten Street), which is from the late 17th century/early 18th century. It is brick and, in some ways, more simple, because the <u>architect</u> has been influenced by classical designs.

St Paul's Cathedral

Tudor townhouse

House from late 17th Century

Get your house in order!

Rewrite this list of buildings in order, from the oldest to the most recent. They are all in this chapter.

St Paul's Cathedral (Christopher Wren's)	
Queen's House, Greenwich	
Oxburgh Hall	
Hardwick Hall	
Hampton Court Palace	

The Tudor part of Hampton Court

Quick on the draw?

Art is all around us. Newspapers contain photographs and cartoons, as well as adverts. You probably have posters up in your room, and there may be pictures on the wall of your house. There are <u>sculptures</u> in shopping centres, in parks and alongside motorways, such as the Angel of the North in the northeast of England.

How was art presented in the period 1485–1750?

Art for everyone?

Many paintings were done for rich <u>patrons</u> and would have ended up in palaces and great houses. However, more ordinary people could see art in lots of ways.

Elizabeth I, Dover Town Hall

- **Paintings in public buildings**: for example, this 1598 painting of Elizabeth I was hung in Dover Town Hall.

- **Religious art in churches**: especially before the Reformation. The opportunity to see art on display in churches was mainly lost after the Reformation, as much of it was destroyed.

- **Images of rulers on coins**.

- **Architecture** (see 'An ideal home?').

- **Woodcuts and engravings**: woodcuts were cheap pictures cut into wood and then printed out. Engravings were a bit more detailed and were made by cutting very fine lines into metal and printing from these. Pictures could be printed off in large numbers. Sometimes, they were illustrations in books, and sometimes they were part of cheap pamphlets and <u>broadsheets</u>, which even quite poor people could afford. Often the pamphlets and broadsheets were designed so that people could understand them even if they didn't read well – because the pictures told the story clearly. This woodcut shown is from a series called 'The dance of death'. It was supposed to show that death came to everyone, even rich people, and was designed by Holbein in 1526.

- **Cartoons**: all sorts of cartoons were to be found in this period. Early on, many made religious points, but later in the period, the political cartoon took off. To us, they can seem quite disgusting, like the 1740 cartoon 'Idol worship, or the way to preferment', which shows people having to kiss Robert Walpole's giant bottom before they can get into Parliament!

Woodcut from 'The dance of death'

Drawing on your knowledge!

Answer the questions to complete the grid.

1	■	D			■							
2		R					■	■	■	■	■	■
3		A					■				■	■
4	■	W					■	■	■	■	■	■

1 A picture of the Day of Judgement
2 He wanted to be painted 'warts and all'
3 He was made court painter to Henry VIII
4 A picture cut into wood and then printed

⬆ At the beginning of this period, religious art was one of the most important types of art. Most pre-Reformation churches were decorated wonderfully, with statues, <u>altar pieces</u> and wall paintings. A particularly dramatic sort of wall painting

Box Hill, Surrey

was the <u>doom picture</u>, which showed the <u>Day of Judgement</u>. The decoration in churches was designed to teach people and encourage their Christian life, but it also gave people a chance to see something that was often beautiful, dramatic or just colourful every week when they went to church. After the Reformation, many statues were removed or destroyed and many wall paintings were covered.

➡ One development of the Renaissance was that painters wanted to paint <u>portraits</u> that looked like the person they represented. Some portrait painters in England existed at the start of the period, but in the 1530s a man came to England who had a big effect on portrait painting. His name was Hans Holbein and he became official court painter to Henry VIII. He painted perhaps the most famous picture of Henry VIII (see 'Tudor "spin" in action'). Tastes changed over the period. For example, while Holbein tried to make his subjects look good, Oliver Cromwell wanted to be painted 'warts and all'. Over this period, England became quite famous for its portraits.

⬇ By the end of the period, landscape painting had become popular. English artists were interested in painting pictures of landscapes, especially the countryside. The 1733 picture of Box Hill, Surrey, painted by George Lambert, is an example.

• TOP TIPS •

When you look at portraits, see if the person is standing on a carpet. Carpets were very expensive in this period and often were hung on walls or used as table coverings, so everyone could see them. People didn't stand on them for fear of spoiling them. If you chose to stand on a carpet in a painting, it meant you were very rich.

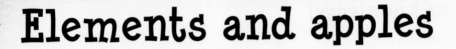

Elements and apples

When you watch the news, you often see an interview with a reporter from the other side of the world. The interview is live, but you can see and hear the reporter on your TV. The picture is probably being sent around the earth with the help of satellites in space.

Satellites like this are designed to circle the earth – just like the moon. We understand the laws of <u>gravity</u>, so we know that satellites will not fly off into space; instead they use the earth's gravity to spin around the earth. Although a satellite wouldn't be put into space for a few hundred years after his birth, Isaac Newton, who was born in 1642, first realised they would work.

Did you know that people in the Middle Ages thought there were only four elements: earth, air, fire and water? In your science lessons, you probably have a copy of the 'periodic table' on the wall. It lists all the elements – from silver and gold to neon and argon. Although Robert Boyle (1627–91) was never able to name any of them, he believed that medieval scientists were wrong, and argued that there were many elements.

Important institutions

The Royal Society was designed to support scientific research. It was set up after the Restoration in 1660, and Charles II was its first patron.

The Royal Observatory was founded at Greenwich in 1675 to observe the stars, but it also aimed to help people find out more about the earth. For example, it was hoped that the observatory would help find a way for sailors to work out <u>longitude</u> when they were at sea.

Many discoveries in the period helped later scientists make their discoveries. Boyle is a good example: he didn't discover the modern elements, but by suggesting they existed, he 'paved the way' for later scientists.

Robert Boyle

Sir Isaac Newton

Naming names!

Under each clue, write down the name of the person being described.

He nearly gave himself permanent eye damage by looking at the sun for an experiment.	He cut up stags from the royal hunt to help his understanding of the blood.	He gave his name to a famous comet.	He realised that not everything could be broken down into the medieval 'four elements'.

KEY FACTS

➡️ **William Harvey (1578–1657):** the court physician to James I and Charles I. Harvey discovered the blood's circulation (in other words, how blood is pumped around the body). Harvey was helped in his research because James I liked hunting: as soon as the royal hunters killed anything, they would let Harvey cut it up to see how it worked!

⬆️ **Robert Hooke (1635–1703):** perhaps best known for Hooke's law, which is about how springs stretch, but he was also interested in microscopes and biology. In fact, Hooke first used the term 'cell' – he said that what he saw in plants under microscopes looked like the cells monks used. Hooke also worked with Christopher Wren to design buildings.

➡️ **Sir Christopher Wren (1632–1723):** an architect, but Wren was also interested in science, especially astronomy, maths and physics. He was one of the first members of the Royal Society.

➡️ **Sir Isaac Newton (1642–1727):** probably most famous for discovering the laws of gravity. He is said to have been sitting under an apple tree when an apple fell from it, and this made him wonder why things always fell straight downwards. He also did lots of important work with maths, mechanics and light. Newton first discovered that white light was a mixture of lots of different colours. He also took a lot of risks in his research – he nearly did permanent damage to his eyes by staring at the sun.

⬇️ **Edmond Halley (1656–1742):** a scientist and astronomer most famous for his work on comets. In 1682, he saw a comet and read what previous astronomers had written about comets. He noticed that 'his' comet was really similar to the comets seen in 1531 and 1607. He predicted it would return in 1757. He was almost correct (though for reasons he couldn't have foreseen, it actually arrived in 1758). The comet is named 'Halley's Comet' after him.

• TOP TIPS •

If you are asked to consider if something was important, try to look at it from a lot of different 'angles'. For example, would people have thought their discoveries were important at the time or is it just when we look back that we see them as important? Were discoveries important because they took science forward and could be applied to other areas of life? For instance, perhaps Christopher Wren owed part of his skill as an architect to his knowledge of science.

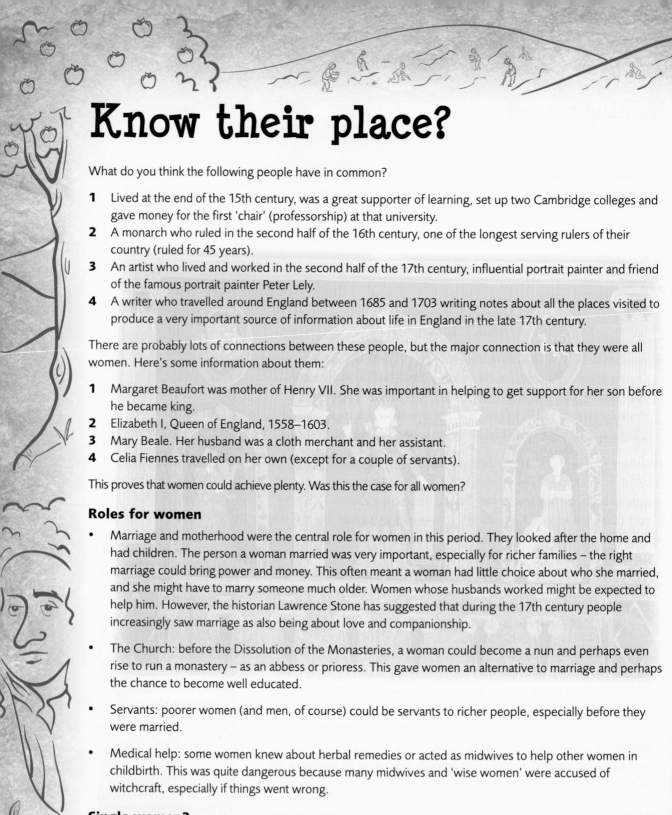

Know their place?

What do you think the following people have in common?

1 Lived at the end of the 15th century, was a great supporter of learning, set up two Cambridge colleges and gave money for the first 'chair' (professorship) at that university.

2 A monarch who ruled in the second half of the 16th century, one of the longest serving rulers of their country (ruled for 45 years).

3 An artist who lived and worked in the second half of the 17th century, influential portrait painter and friend of the famous portrait painter Peter Lely.

4 A writer who travelled around England between 1685 and 1703 writing notes about all the places visited to produce a very important source of information about life in England in the late 17th century.

There are probably lots of connections between these people, but the major connection is that they were all women. Here's some information about them:

1 Margaret Beaufort was mother of Henry VII. She was important in helping to get support for her son before he became king.

2 Elizabeth I, Queen of England, 1558–1603.

3 Mary Beale. Her husband was a cloth merchant and her assistant.

4 Celia Fiennes travelled on her own (except for a couple of servants).

This proves that women could achieve plenty. Was this the case for all women?

Roles for women

- Marriage and motherhood were the central role for women in this period. They looked after the home and had children. The person a woman married was very important, especially for richer families – the right marriage could bring power and money. This often meant a woman had little choice about who she married, and she might have to marry someone much older. Women whose husbands worked might be expected to help him. However, the historian Lawrence Stone has suggested that during the 17th century people increasingly saw marriage as also being about love and companionship.

- The Church: before the Dissolution of the Monasteries, a woman could become a nun and perhaps even rise to run a monastery – as an abbess or prioress. This gave women an alternative to marriage and perhaps the chance to become well educated.

- Servants: poorer women (and men, of course) could be servants to richer people, especially before they were married.

- Medical help: some women knew about herbal remedies or acted as midwives to help other women in childbirth. This was quite dangerous because many midwives and 'wise women' were accused of witchcraft, especially if things went wrong.

Single women?

Women were expected to get married, but there were some single women. A survey in Ealing in 1599 suggested that about a quarter of women aged between 40 and 70 years had never married. Widows could be quite powerful because they might have a lot of money or run their dead husband's business. Some women were single because their husbands had left them. In 1570, a survey of the poor in Norwich discovered that about 7% of poor women had been deserted by their husbands.

Woman wise!

True or **false**.

1   A nickname for a bossy wife was 'mouse'.

2   A midwife could be accused of witchcraft.

3   A woman could not become monarch.

4   All women married.

KEY FACTS

Primogeniture

⬆ This means that important things such as noble titles, or even kingdoms, are passed on to the eldest child. For example, the Duke of Norfolk's land, and his title, would pass to his eldest child, but this child had to be a male – women could not inherit titles. A woman could become queen of England, but only if there were no close male heirs. This is why Mary I only became queen after her younger brother Edward died.

Double standards?

➡ Henry VIII had many mistresses and children with them and made little attempt to hide these affairs. One of his children, Henry Fitzroy, even became Duke of Richmond in the 1520s. His surname made it clear who he was – Fitz means '<u>illegitimate</u> son' and 'roy' is from the French word meaning 'king', so his name was 'Henry, illegitimate son of the king'. In contrast, two of Henry's wives were executed because of suspected affairs with other men. In general, a wife's affairs were treated more harshly than a husband's. This seems unfair, but it did have a purpose. The man, who might have money, land or even a kingdom to pass to his sons, needed to know that it was his son that inherited. If his wife had affairs, he couldn't be sure.

Childbirth

⬇ In this period before antibiotics and disinfectants, giving birth was very dangerous, and many women died in childbirth.

Shrews

⬆ Women who bossed their husbands about were sometimes known as 'shrews'. William Shakespeare wrote a play called *The Taming of the Shrew*, in which a husband does terrible things to his wife to stop her being so bossy. If you watch this play, it can seem really unfair, but at the time people would have thought it was funny.

• TOP TIPS •

When you write about women, don't just talk about famous women like Elizabeth I. Remember to talk about the life of ordinary women and remember that things are never simple – there are usually exceptions to the rule. For example, although women had to obey their husbands, some husbands allowed their wives a lot of freedom and although women were expected to marry, there were some single women at this time.

Childhood? What childhood?

You probably spend a lot of your weekdays at school, and you may choose to stay in full-time education beyond the age of 16. Education up to 18 is probably free, unless you attend a fee-paying school. You might have a part-time job, like a paper round, and you may help out a bit at home, but you probably also have free time to do things you enjoy.

How different would your life have been in the early modern period? To start with, you would have had a much lower chance of surviving at all as <u>infant mortality</u> was very high. You would probably have had more brothers and sisters than today, as families tended to be larger. The sort of life you lived would depend on your social class and whether you were a boy or girl.

- **Child of a noble:** educated at home, by tutors. Each person's education would have been different, but you would probably have been taught several languages, some history and some philosophy, as well as how to play a musical instrument. You were more likely to be educated if you were a boy, but some girls were educated (Elizabeth I and Sir Thomas More's daughters had excellent educations). By 13, however, boys would probably be in the service of a noble or other great man to get experience of life in a great <u>household</u>. Really lucky boys or girls might have visited the royal court. You might already be engaged to be married (usually arranged by your parents). At the age of 15, Catherine Howard, for example, was married to Henry VIII, who was 49 at the time!

- **Child of a well-off merchant:** especially by the end of the Tudor period, you might have gone to a grammar school. Hours were very long, and beatings were frequent. Only boys tended to go to grammar school; but, towards the end of the period, girls were going to school more.

- **Child of a poorer person:** Boys particularly would probably have worked in the fields or been apprenticed by the age of 13, so they could learn a craft or trade. Some girls would also have been apprentices until they married. Children of vagrants (see 'Not all banquets and dancing'), may have been forced into apprenticeships.

Schools up!

It's your turn to be the teacher! Find the mistakes in this pieces of writing and correct them.
(There are six mistakes.)

1 Most children went to school in this period. Some children were educated at home, for example Thomas More's daughters. They had a very bad home education.

2 Children could become apprentices instead of going to school. Their masters were not allowed to beat them.

3 Children could be married very young, for example Katherine Parr was 12 when she married the 30-year-old Henry VIII.

KEY FACTS

Childhood?

In many ways, a childhood as we know it didn't exist:

↗ Children would begin their adult life very young, often starting work before their tenth birthday and marrying when they were still in their teens.

→ This was a harsh period – a time of plague, illness and poverty for many ordinary people. Children were needed to help support their families. Even richer children needed to be trained in the kind of life they were going to lead and to help keep their families rich and powerful.

Training

Even if many people did not go to school, there was still a lot of training:

↓ Apprentices would learn a trade or a craft. Apprentices were assigned to their master for a number of years, and the master could treat them pretty much as he wanted. There are examples of masters – and mistresses – being pardoned if they beat their apprentices to death, although, fortunately, not every apprentice was treated so badly.

↗ Parents would train their children in relevant skills – a girl might learn needlework or cooking.

Yobs?

↖ Today, many people say that young people's behaviour is bad, and people worry that young people form groups and cause trouble on the streets. This is not the first time that people worried about violent young people – apprentices were often in trouble for causing mayhem. In 1516, for example, a group of London apprentices tried to murder a man and then went on to vandalise a shop.

• TOP TIPS •

In this chapter, you've compared the experiences of children in this period with your own experiences. When you are making comparisons, make sure you mention the two things you are comparing. For example, 'Schools in early modern England cost money for most children, **whereas today** in England every child has the right to free schooling'.

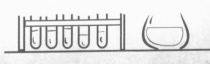

Test your knowledge 5

This assessment aims to help you to:

*   argue a case

*   structure your thoughts

*   see things from different viewpoints – our modern viewpoint and the period under study's viewpoint

*   review your understanding of the role of women in the period.

You are going to answer the question, 'Were women oppressed in the Tudor period?'

Task 1: arguments that suggest women were oppressed
Choose anything from 'Know their place?' (or anywhere else) that suggests women were oppressed. Make sure you give examples whenever you can. The following are some thoughts, but you can say what you like:

*   patriarchal system

*   women who did speak their mind could be called 'shrews'

*   limited career opportunities for most women.

....
....
....
....
....
....

(10 marks)

Task 2: arguments that suggest women were not oppressed
Choose anything from 'Know their place?' (or anywhere else) that suggests women were not oppressed. Make sure that you give examples whenever you can. The following are some thoughts, but you can say what you like:

*   some women were really powerful (including five queens in England and Scotland – Mary I, Elizabeth I, Mary, Queen of Scots, Mary II and Queen Anne)

*   many people, both women and men, were 'oppressed' in this period, e.g. very few people had the vote and many people lived a 'subsistence' lifestyle (in other words, only having enough just to feed their family, with nothing to spare).

....
....
....

- **very important**: do we judge the period by our own standards? Would women of that era have seen themselves as oppressed? Could we say that, at the time, these things were part of the way things were?

....

....

....

....

....

....

(10 marks)

Task 3: your conclusion

What is your overall view? Why? Make sure you make the final decision when you've mentioned a point in both sections. For example, is it more important that **some** women were powerful or that **many** women had quite limited opportunities outside the home?

....

....

....

....

(5 marks)

What to do next

You could write this up into a piece of extended writing. If you do this, you will need to include an introduction. Here are some top tips for introductions:

- Say what the key words mean, e.g. oppressive, as this will help you to really focus in the rest of your piece.

- As you already know what you're going to argue, you can set up a point to knock it down. For instance, if you think women **were** oppressed, the introduction could say something like, 'We might think that women were very important in this period, because England and Scotland had five queens; however, most women were not as powerful as this'. If you don't think women were oppressed, you could say something like, 'We might look at the limited roles of women in this period and think that they were oppressed; however, this would be because we would mainly look at things from a modern viewpoint rather than an early modern perspective.'

(Total 25 marks)

Not all banquets and dancing

Do you sometimes imagine what it would have been like to have lived in this period? You might imagine being at the royal court, wearing fine clothes and attending parties, being a soldier or servant in a great household or being a farmer or a merchant with a shop selling books, food or spices from distant lands.

Do you ever imagine what it would have been like to be really poor? The period had no national health service, no job centres and no unemployment benefit. If you became ill and you either had no parents to care for you, or your parents couldn't afford to look after you, you might have been lucky and been looked after by a monastery, but you might have had to become a beggar. A woman or a child who became ill would have had more chance of being looked after, but a man who lost his job and was not ill, probably wouldn't have got help from anyone. This is because people in 1485 thought there were enough jobs for everyone – they believed anyone without a job was lazy.

You could sometimes be punished for poverty. In 1547, Edward VI's government passed a very harsh law designed to deal with vagrants. (In 1547, anyone who didn't have a job for more than three days was classed as a vagrant.)

Vagrancy Act, 1547

- *A person convicted of being a vagrant for the first time was branded with a 'V'. He was then handed into slavery for two years – often with the person who reported him. When the person was a slave, he had to do anything his master wanted, which, of course, meant that slaves could be treated very badly.*

  - *A runaway slave was made a slave for life – if he ran away again, he was executed.*

- *The children of vagrants could be snatched away by anyone prepared to teach them a trade. Boys would be apprenticed until they were 24 years old and girls until they were 20. The person who seized them did not have to discuss it with their parents, and, of course, the children had no choice. Runaway apprentices would be made slaves. Parents who tried to get their children back could also be made slaves.*

This act was just one attempt made by a government to solve the problem of poverty. It was seen as so harsh that it was cancelled in 1550. However, many other things were done by governments to try to deal with poverty.

The monasteries

The monasteries also did a lot to help the poor – they would often give them food, money and medical help. Any traveller, however poor, could get food and shelter at a monastery. Sometimes, the sons of the poor were even educated. When Henry VIII closed the monasteries, this source of help was lost. Some historians think this is why the governments had to start passing more laws to deal with the problems of poverty.

Helping the poor?

Unscramble the following anagrams to make words or phrases from this chapter.

1 TANGRAV

2 BAND RING

3 RECLUSE NO

3 TREASON IS ME

5 BALLERINA WEPT HAS ZOO

KEY FACTS

Government action to deal with poverty

◁ In the early Tudor period, some acts tried to deal with the problem of poverty. They tended to focus on stopping vagrancy and illegal begging, but very little was done to help healthy people who couldn't find work. However, some laws were passed against <u>enclosure</u>, which many people thought caused poverty.

▷ The first act that hinted at making people pay to help the poor was in 1552. The act said that any richer people who refused to give money for the poor could be sent to the bishop to be told off.

▽ Some of the most important action taken was in the Elizabethan period, when the Poor Laws were passed. These were some of the first laws to recognise that there wasn't always work for people who wanted it. The Elizabethan Poor Laws still had lots of punishments for people who were felt to be 'undeserving' and deliberately lazy, but they also set up workhouses, so that people could be put to work. They said that people should be taxed to pay for poor relief.

△ In 1662, the Acts of Settlement meant that people had to live in the parish in which they were born to get poor relief, because each parish was responsible for deciding how much money they should give the poor. Some poor people had travelled around looking for the most generous parishes, and the Acts of Settlement were designed to stop this.

• TOP TIPS •

If you are asked whether something changed, try to show both sides of the picture. For instance, if you are asked what changed in the government's treatment of the poor, you might say that the governments always punished some people for poverty, but over this period, they brought more laws in to help people who wanted to work but couldn't.

Plague and putrefaction

'Ring a ring o' roses,
A pocket full of posies
A-tishoo, a-tishoo
We all fall down'

This popular nursery rhyme sounds quite pretty, but it is about one of the nastiest diseases ever to hit England, in 1665.

The plague was a horrible disease; symptoms started with a red rash (*ring of roses*), sneezing (*a-tishoo*), fevers and swellings and eventually a painful death (*we all fall down*). The plague was carried by fleas, which lived on rats. It was worsened by the dirt in streets and houses and on people (who rarely washed), which attracted rats. People ran away from London to avoid the plague, but instead they dispersed it around the country because they carried plague fleas. The plague was not a new disease, in 1602, 30 000 died; however, the outbreak in 1665 was the worst, killing 65 000 people. With so many deaths, bodies were put in mass graves called 'plague pits'.

People had no idea how the plague spread. Many thought it was bad air (miasma), so they held bunches of flowers (*pocket full of posies*) to their noses to avoid it. This didn't stop the plague. People did understand that someone with the plague could pass it to other people, so when someone starting showing the symptoms, they, and everyone in their house, were banned from going outside.

The Great Plague of 1665 was winding down by the summer of 1666 but might easily have broken out again because the unhealthy conditions were still there. This is why the Great Fire of London, which destroyed so much of the city, was probably a good thing. With the houses and streets it destroyed, it also killed the plague rats.

Other unpleasant diseases that were common at this time were smallpox, which could be <u>fatal</u> (and those who did survive were often horribly scarred), and typhus, which was spread by lice and fleas.

Did things change much in this period?

- Some changes in understanding happened. Harvey discovered the blood's circulation (see 'Elements and apples'), Vesalius developed the understanding of anatomy in his 1543 book and Paré made discoveries about surgery. Their ideas were slow to catch on in practice, however – most doctors still believed in the four humours (see Key Facts).

- Some changes in technology happened. Sanctorius (1561–1636) was first to use a simple thermometer to take temperatures. Again, these ideas took time to catch on.

- England had very few trained physicians, so new ideas took even longer to take effect.

- Many people still preferred the old ideas. Harvey, for example, lost patients after he published his theories about blood's circulation – people thought he was mad!

- <u>Sanitation</u> was still very poor. <u>Sewage</u> was pumped into the Thames, and people became ill because they took their drinking water from the river.

- At the end of this period, English surgeons emphasised their difference from barbers. In 1745, they broke away from the Company of Barber Surgeons (founded in 1540) to found the Company of Surgeons.

Plaguing puzzles

Draw a line to link each disease with its description.

Last major European outbreak in 1665. Carried by fleas on rats	Smallpox
A non-fatal skin disease, which peopled believed would be cured if it was touched by the English king	Typhus
Named for the Greek word typhos, meaning 'hazy'. Spread by lice and fleas.	Plague
Often fatal. Left survivors with very nasty scars	Scrofula

KEY FACTS

Some common treatments

⬆ **Bloodletting was popular and was based on the idea that the body was made up of four 'humours': choler (yellow bile), blood, phlegm and melancholy (black bile). People thought that cutting someone to let them bleed might restore the balance between the humours, which was needed to keep well. This carried on even after Harvey discovered the blood's circulation.**

➡ **Surgery took place without anaesthetics, so it was avoided if possible. One favourite method for sealing a wound after surgery was cauterisation – a 500-year-old procedure that meant burning the scar. Some people, such as the French surgeon Paré, had made discoveries that would improve surgery, but they were slow to catch on.**

⬇ **Leeches were used on the same principle as bloodletting. A leech would suck out some of the blood to restore the balance of the humours**

⬆ **Where would you have gone for treatment? Here is a list of places you might have gone to. See the glossary at the back for more detail.**

- **Hospital**
- **Apothecary**
- **Wise woman**
- **Barber surgeon**
- **Physician**
- **Asylum**
- **Quack**
- **The monarch (people believed that being touched by the English king could cure a skin disease called scrofula).**

• TOP TIPS •

Imagine you have been asked to think about how effective the treatment of disease was. Think about what might be meant by 'effective'. Does it mean that few people died? Does it mean improvements happened? Does it mean that it was as good as it could have been under the circumstances? It might mean all of these – looking at the question from different angles like this is always impressive.

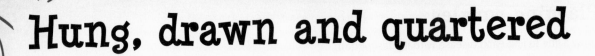

Hung, drawn and quartered

People have very strong views about crime and punishment. If you ask someone today whether they think the current treatment of criminals is fair, it is likely they either will think it is not fair because it is too harsh or they will think it is not tough enough.

Can you guess the official punishment for the crimes described below?

1   A priest convicted of murder in 1500.

2   Someone convicted of heresy who will not <u>repent</u> of their heresy.

3   A <u>commoner</u> convicted of stealing property worth 13d in 1580.

4   A vagrant convicted of a first offence in 1549.

5   A woman convicted of witchcraft.

6   A commoner convicted of serious crimes against the state, such as treason.

Here are typical punishments for these crimes:

1   Branding on the thumb with an 'M', perhaps also imprisonment. Priests and other members of the church could claim 'benefit of clergy' – they would be tried by church courts, from which punishments were less harsh. A law passed in 1489 meant they were also branded and that benefit could only be claimed once. After 1576, clergy were tried for crimes in ordinary courts, although they could still get a lighter punishment. By the end of this period, benefit of clergy ceased being for clergymen only – it became a way to get lighter punishments for a first offence.

2   Burning at the stake for all social classes. A person convicted of a first offence who repented would be let off burning. If they were convicted again, they would probably be executed – even if they did repent.

3   Death by hanging. Anyone caught stealing property worth over 12d (a shilling) could be punished by death. In practice, however, people were often not executed – a judge might deliberately value the property stolen at less than 12d.

4   Branding with a 'V' and slavery for two years. This law of 1547 was seen as harsh even at the time and was soon changed (see 'All banquets and dancing').

5   Hanging.

6   This person would be hung, drawn and quartered. This is a really gruesome method of killing, so skip the next bit if you are squeamish! A person was hung but taken down before they were dead. They were cut open at the front of their body and their guts pulled out while they were alive (drawn). They were then cut into pieces (quartered). Nobles convicted of treason had it relatively easy in comparison – they were beheaded (had their heads cut off).

Criticisms

Not everyone thought the system of punishment in this period was good. Thomas More was a politician and writer, who was executed when he refused to accept Henry VIII as head of the Church of England. In his book, *Utopia* (1516), his major character argues that it is stupid to execute someone for stealing. The character says that if someone is going to be executed for stealing someone's money, they might as well kill the person they are stealing from so that person can't testify against them. In this way, the law is encouraging more killing.

Highwaymen

During this period, it was very dangerous to travel, as people could attack you, steal your money and possibly kill you. The most famous criminals of this type were 'highwaymen'. Towards the end of this period, people travelled a lot in stage coaches. Highwaymen would 'hold up' stage coaches and steal money from the people inside. The most famous highwayman is probably Dick Turpin. He was caught and was hanged in York in 1739.

Pirates

Pirates committed crimes at sea. One of the most famous pirates was Edward Teach, or 'Blackbeard'. He was executed in 1718 and his head mounted on a pole as a warning to others. Some pirates were semi-official. For example, Francis Drake under Elizabeth I was a 'privateer'. He had an official licence to rob Spanish treasure ships, as long as he passed a good amount of what he stole to Queen Elizabeth I!

Witches

Many people in Europe at this time were accused of witchcraft. They were mainly old women, although some men were also accused. In comparison with some other countries, England executed relatively few witches, but some people were convicted. In East Anglia in the mid-17th century, a man called Matthew Hopkins, who called himself the 'Witchfinder General', was responsible for the death of many people successfully charged with witchcraft.

Hangagrams

Unscramble these anagrams. They are all names of people mentioned in this chapter.

1	METHINKS APT HOW	
2	CABLED BARK	
3	SIDECAR FRANK	
4	HANDIWORK ATE HER	
5	PUTRID NICK	

KEY FACTS

⬆ In this period, most executions were held in public – many <u>felons</u> in London were executed on Tower Hill. People would go to watch these executions, which were often seen as entertainment. Some people were executed privately to protect them from this: the two wives of Henry VIII who were executed (Anne Boleyn and Catherine Howard) were executed inside the Tower of London.

· TOP TIPS ·

When deciding what punishment you think would be fair in the 21st century, consider what you know about the period 1485–1750. In a period with very limited policing, is there an argument that punishments had to be harsher than now to help control crime?

Test your knowledge 6

This assessment aims to help you to:

• review what you have learnt through this whole book

• develop your skills of comparing and contrasting.

Task 1
Complete the two tables below to show as many similarities and differences between the British Isles in 1485 and in 1750. All the chapters on England, Wales, Scotland and Ireland will help you. You might even find some things in the European chapters. There are lots of topics you might want to think about, but here are some examples:

• *life of women*	• *art, architecture and science*
• *life of children*	• *the Church*
• *treatment of the poor*	• *Ireland*
• *power of Parliament*	• *Scotland*
• *power of the monarchy*	• *Wales*
• *treatment of crime*	• *the creation of a 'united kingdom'.*
• *the theatre*	

Similarities between 1485 and 1750	
1485	**1750**
Example: • England ruled by monarchs	Example: • England ruled by monarchs

Differences between 1485 and 1750	
1485	1750
Example: • England and Scotland were two independent countries with different monarchs.	Example: • England and Scotland were ruled by the same monarch and there had been an Act of Union (1707) joining the two countries.

(20 marks)

Task 2

How different do you think the British Isles in 1750 were from the British Isles in 1485? Now that you've filled in the charts, draw a conclusion:

....

....

....

....

(10 marks)

(Total 30 marks)

Glossary

Abdicate To give up being king or queen.

Accession to the throne Becoming monarch.

Allied When people or countries work together or support each other.

Altar piece A painting or other piece of art designed to go on an altar (a table at the end of a medieval church, where much of the church service happened).

Apothecary Apothecaries were like modern pharmacists, but they weren't trained. Some treatments they gave were very good, but some could do real harm.

Architect Designer of buildings.

Asylum The families of mentally ill people might have sent them to an asylum, such as St Mary of Bethlem ('Bedlam'), London.

Barber surgeon In this period surgery was separate from medicine, and the local barber was usually also a surgeon. Barber surgeons could be very skilled, but surgery was still very dangerous.

Baroque 17th-century style of art and architecture. Its main focus was on being dramatic and almost 'over the top'.

Branded When a hot piece of iron, which could be shaped as a mark or letter, was used to burn a mark into the skin.

Broadsheet A large sheet of paper, printed on one side. They were cheap to produce and often contained gossip, odd stories and pictures.

Civil war A war that takes place in one country, where both sides come from that country.

Clan Group of Scottish Highlanders who were all part of, or followers of, the same family group.

Classical Describes the ancient Greek and Roman style of art, literature and culture and more modern things that follow that style.

Colonists A group of people from one country who live in another country (colony) but are ruled by their original country.

Commoner An ordinary person – not a noble.

Dauphin The title of the oldest son of the King of France.

Day of Judgement The day when God will judge all people. Christianity is one religion that has a Day of Judgement. An old world for the Christian Day of Judgement is Domesday ('doom's day').

Depose To take a position of power away from someone – to depose a king is to stop them being king.

Diet The assembly of the Holy Roman Empire (like a parliament).

Diocese Area that a bishop oversees, also sometimes called a see or bishopric.

Discipline In the Council of Trent, discipline didn't necessarily mean punishment. It meant setting rules and keeping things in order.

Discalced Barefoot or wearing only sandals.

Dissolution of the monasteries Closure of the monasteries.

Doctrine Official religious belief.

Doom picture/doom painting Picture of the Day of Judgement, showing some people going to heaven and some to hell. It was designed to make people live a good Christian life.

Elector Person who votes. In the Holy Roman Empire, the Electors were seven princes and archbishops who chose the new emperor.

Empire This word has two meanings: a place ruled by an emperor or a collection of overseas territories ruled by one country.

Enclosure Fencing off land. Farmers might fence off land previously used by everyone (common land) or they might buy lots of farms and make them into one big farm (engrossing). A lot of people thought enclosure and engrossing contributed to job losses.

Exclusion To be excluded is to be left out.

Exposed timbers Timbers are large pieces of wood – like large planks. Exposed timbers (in a building) can be seen and are both 'structural' and 'decorative' (unlike structural timbers that just hold up buildings, and are covered up).

Fatal Something that can kill you.

Felony A crime punishable by death. Someone committing a felony was known as a felon.

Fortified Made safe – like a castle. Semi-fortified means that it was fortified a little – like Oxburgh Hall.

Golden Age A mythical perfect time when everyone is happy, healthy and wealthy.

Gravity The force of attraction between any object in the Earth's gravitational field and the Earth itself.

Heir Your heir is the person who will get your things when you die. If you have a title, such as king, they will usually get this too.

Heresies Beliefs that are different from official beliefs and are considered to be wrong.

Heretic Someone whose religious beliefs are seen as heresies. Mary, as a Catholic, believed that Protestants were heretics. Edward, as a Protestant, believed that Catholics were heretics.

Hermit A person who lives on their own, away from people, and spends most of their time praying.

Highlands The northern, mountainous part of Scotland.

Holy Land Term used to refer to modern-day Israel/Palestine.

Holy Roman Empire Empire in central Europe ruled by the Holy Roman Emperor. It included much of modern-day Germany and Austria.

Hospital Some charity hospitals were run by the Church, but many were monastic and were shut down with the dissolution of the monasteries. By the end of the period, several large towns had set up hospitals; however, they were not free.

Household Group of people in one house. A noble household would include many family members and servants. It would often also include other young nobles or members of the gentry.

Illegitimate Term describing a child born to unmarried parents, who would often not have inherited their father's money, land or titles.

Independence The ability to act as you want to. When Scotland was independent from England, it didn't have to do what England wanted.

Industrial revolution A time when things started to be made in factories rather than people's homes. The factories made things on a much larger scale, and the machines were usually powered by steam engines. New discoveries, mainly in the later 18th and 19th centuries, helped this to take place.

Infant mortality The number of babies or very young children who died.

Intercede To ask something on behalf of someone else. Catholics believed that because the saints were in heaven, they could talk to God on behalf of a Christian on earth.

Landscape A view of things on land, such as hills or woods. There might even be a town or city in a landscape. The same thing of the sea is called a 'seascape'.

Lay Anyone not belonging to the clergy (e.g. a priest or a monk) is a lay person. Non-clergy are known as the 'laity'.

Lease A contract in which you use or occupy something for a set period of time only.

Legitimate A child whose parents were married and who could therefore inherit the father's money, land or titles.

Life expectancy The average number of years that people live for.

Literate Being able to read and write. It is hard to work out rates of literacy in this period – often historians just have to use the number of people who could sign their name. However, relatively few people were literate.

Longitude Lines of longitude are imaginary lines that run around the earth from north to south. They are especially useful for sailors working out where they are at sea.

Mass A service celebrating the death and resurrection of Jesus and his sacrifice for the world. Also called 'Eucharist'. Protestants call it 'Holy Communion' or 'the Lord's Supper'.

Massacre The killing of a huge number of people.

Mechanics A branch of physics that deals with the effects of energy and forces of the motion of physical objects.

Monarch The ruler (king or queen) of a country.

Monarchy A country ruled by a monarch (king or queen) or a way of describing the kingship as a whole and not just an individual king (e.g.' the monarchy was weak').

Monk A man who gives his life to join a group of other men to pray and worship God together. They usually live together in a monastery, although sometimes they work in the 'world'. Luther, for instance, worked in a university. A female monk is called a nun. Luther believed that people should not be monks or nuns.

Noble A person of high birth or someone with a title, such as the Duke of Suffolk or the Earl of Surrey. Noble families were very important and often very rich. The king needed them as supporters, but they could be dangerous if they turned against a king.

Nonconformist Someone who does not conform (i.e. do what they are told to do). Religious nonconformists in this period were Protestants who went to a church other than the Church of England.

Opera A play in which all, or most, of the words, are sung. Opera was probably invented in 1597 in the Italian town of Florence.

Oppressive Cruel, harsh or depressing.

Pagan There are lots of different meanings to this word. It can mean the religion before Christianity or the worship of spirits and the natural world.

Pale A small area of Ireland that English kings controlled directly; it included Dublin and the land around it.

Papacy The rule of the popes (the leader of the Catholic Church is called the Pope) or the general job rather than an individual pope (e.g. 'the papacy was weak').

Parish Area that a parish priest oversees.

Parliament Group of men who represented the country. Some were elected, and some were nobles and bishops. The king needed a Parliament if he wanted to tax his people or pass laws.

Patriarchal The word 'patriarch' comes from the Christian and Jewish scriptures, where it refers to male religious leaders. It is often used to describe any sort of male in charge, such as the head of a family. The word patriarchal is used to describe a system or a society in which men are in charge. For instance, early modern Europe was a patriarchal society.

Patron A person who gives support to something or someone.

Physician The forerunner of our modern medical doctor although not as knowledgeable, as many important discoveries, for example understanding the effects of germs, had not been made.

Pilgrimage A special journey to a holy place. Pilgrimages were often the only chance people had to travel.

Plantation The English government's policy of 'planting' colonies of Protestants in Ireland to try to control the Irish.

Political To do with government.

Portrait A painting of a person at this time.

Pre-eminence To be pre-eminent is to come before everyone else, to be the most important or to have the most power.

Principality A place ruled by a prince (as opposed to a kingdom ruled by a king or an empire ruled by an emperor).

Protectorate A place ruled by a lord protector. Cromwell was Lord Protector of England.

Protestantism A new type of Christianity that developed during the 16th century. Some religious thinkers, such as Martin Luther in Germany, began to disagree with the Catholic Church. When the Church wouldn't accept their ideas, they formed their own churches.

Puritans Passionate Protestants. The word started as an insult and came from the idea that they were trying to make the Church pure.

Quacks They were regarded as frauds, offering cures that they knew would not work in order to make money.

Reformation The attempt to reform the Catholic Church in 16th-century Europe that led to the formation of Protestant Churches.

Regent Someone who ruled the country on behalf of someone else. Often someone was a regent for a king or queen who was too young to rule.

Relic The remains of something. Holy relics were things linked to saints or Jesus. For instance, lots of cathedrals and monasteries had the bones of saints.

Religious order A group of religious people who form a community and agree to obey a set of rules. Monks are members of religious orders, as are some priests. The Pope has to give his permission for a Catholic order to be set up.

Renaissance Means rebirth. The Renaissance in this period was a big change in ideas and art and took a lot of inspiration from the classical (Greek and Roman) past.

Repent To be sorry for what you have done.

Republic A state not governed by a monarch: power lies with the people and the representatives they elect.

Restoration The re-establishment of the monarchy in Britain in 1660, when Charles II became king.

Revolution A massive change. (In this period, it could also mean 'going around in a circle', so a revolution could be going back to the way things used to be a long time ago).

Roman Catholicism A type of Christianity (sometimes just called Catholicism). The leader of the Roman Catholic Church was the Pope in Rome. At the start of the Tudor period, most of Europe was Catholic.

Sabbath Jewish and Christian holy day. For most Christians, the Sabbath is Sunday, but the Jewish Sabbath (which is where Christians took the term from) is Saturday.

Saint For medieval Catholics, a dead Christian who is now in heaven because of their holy life. Luther would later say that all Christians should be called saints, not just a few especially 'holy' people.

Sanitation Good sanitation is all about keeping healthy conditions, such as clean water, a good air supply and the proper disposal of sewage.

Scripture Holy book. When Christians talk about Scripture, they mean the Bible.

Sculptures Three-dimensional pieces of art.

See Area that a bishop oversees. Sometimes also called a diocese or bishopric.

Sewage Used water and solids carried in water.

Spanish Armada A big fleet of Spanish ships. The most famous came to attack England in 1588.

St Peter and his successors The Popes.

Standing army A regular army that is always there and ready to fight if needed.

Stillborn Term to describe a baby that died before or during birth.

Stuart period Period ruled by monarchs from the Stuart family. It was broken in the middle by the Commonwealth and Protectorate, when England was a republic.

Succession Succession means following on in order (e.g. a son might succeed his father as king) – it also means the right to succeed someone as king.

Suspend To stop for the time being.

Symbol Something that stands for something else. An example of a modern visual symbol is the Nike flash.

Temporal Of the world, as opposed to of God.

Theologians People who learnt about and taught theology. In this period, theologians would probably have studied only the Christian faith.

Theology The study of things to do with God.

Trading station A place in which buying and selling took place. British ships would arrive with goods from home and would then be stocked with things to go back to Britain. They were often like small towns. People lived there permanently to help the trade and might explore the surrounding areas. Trading stations were usually protected – like small forts.

Treason Committing a crime against monarch or country.

Tyranny A system ruled by a tyrant (a ruler who does what they like and often uses force to get their way).

United Things joined together to make them one thing. If people are united, they tend to agree on things and work together.

Vagrant Different periods used the term in slightly different ways, but a vagrant was normally a homeless person.

Wise woman These were local women in villages who knew some herbal remedies. It was a dangerous occupation because if you got things wrong, people were likely to start accusing you of witchcraft!

Answers

Tudorgrams p5

1 Anne Boleyn
2 Spanish Armada
3 Elizabeth
4 Henry

The truth about the Stuarts p7

1 False – James I was already King of <u>Scotland</u> before he became King of England.
2 False – the Gunpowder Plot involved a group of <u>Catholics</u> who tried to blow up Parliament.
3 False – Charles I had an older brother called <u>Henry</u>.
4 False – James II was Charles I's son and was brother to Charles II.
5 True – Charles II became a Catholic on his deathbed.

Setting the date! p9

Glorious Revolution (1688–89)
Start of Nine Years War (1688)
Accession of Queen Anne (1702)
Accession of George I (1714)
First Jacobite Rebellion (1715)
Walpole becomes first Prime Minister (Lord Treasurer) (1722)
Accession of George II (1727)
'Start' of Methodism (1738)
Second Jacobite Rebellion (1745)

Tudorsearch p13

I am... p15

Charles V, Henry VIII, Catherine of Aragon, Anne Boleyn

Mary matters p17

1 about 280   2 111   3 False (see glossary)
4 Philip of Spain   5 Wyatt   6 about £90 000 a year

Puzzling paintings p19

Symbol	Meaning
Pelican	Self-sacrifice
Pearls	Purity
Sieve	Purity
Dog	Faithfulness
Olive branch	Peace

Civil warring p21

1 False   2 True   3 False   4 True   5 False   6 True

Just punishment? p23

1 Yes   2 Yes   3 No   4 No   5 No   6 Yes   7 No – (being drunk was the problem, not the actual alcohol)

Rights or not? p25

1 Right – the monarch cannot raise taxes without Parliament's permission
2 Right – the monarch cannot marry a Catholic
3 Not – the monarch can't have a standing army without <u>Parliament's permission</u>
4 Right – the monarch cannot try to stop free speech in Parliament
5 Not – monarchs stayed until death, unless they abdicated

First or second placed?

First rebellion	Second rebellion
• The Fifteen	• The Forty Five
• James Edward Stuart	• Charles Edward Stuart
• Battle of Preston	• Bonnie Prince Charlie
• Battle of Sheriffmuir	• The Young Pretender
• The Old Pretender	• Battle of Prestonpans
	• Battle of Culloden

Praying people p31

1 Alexander VI
2 Julius II
3 Erasmus
4 Chaucer

Lutheran lessons p33

1 miner
2 a group set up by Protestant leaders to protect themselves from Catholic attack
3 an assembly representing the Holy Roman Empire (see glossary)
4 Elector of Saxony
5 Holy Roman Emperor (Charles V)
6 the Pope
7 there are lots, but the one in the text is Nuremberg
8 follower of Luther's ideas

Mistaken statements p35

1 Pope ~~Pius V~~ **Adrian VI** wanted to reform the Catholic Church but died (in 1523) before he could really do anything.
2 The Council of Trent started meeting in 1545. This was ~~before~~ **after** Martin Luther nailed his 95 theses to the door.
3 An inquisition had been set up in ~~Germany~~ **Spain** in 1478 to deal with Jewish people who had converted to Christianity.
4 A hermit is a person who lives ~~with lots of other people~~ **on their own** so that they can ~~party~~ **pray**. (see glossary)
5 The original Jesuits wanted to go to ~~Germany~~ **the Holy Land** to convert ~~Protestants~~ **Muslims and Jews**.

Sussed your Scots? p39

Mary of Guise, James IV, James VI, Mary Queen of Scots (Mary Stuart), James V

Grasped your Gaelic? p41

1 see descriptions on page 40
2 Lord Deputy of Ireland
3 colonies of Protestants 'planted' in Ireland by the English government to control the Irish
4 a massacre by Oliver Cromwell's troops

Union links p43

Act of Union between Wales and England	1603
Act of Union between Scotland and England	1541
English kings start calling themselves kings of Ireland	1485
James VI of Scotland becomes King James I of England	1536
Henry Tudor (a Welsh noble) becomes King of England	1707

Empire events p45

1 1627   2 1497   3 1620   4 1664   5 1655   6 1690

Theatrical antics p49

1 getting a roof which sheltered audiences from the rain
2 The Alchemist
3 True

Get your house in order! p51

Oxburgh Hall, Hampton Court Palace, Hardwick Hall, Queen's House, Greenwich, St Paul's Cathedral (Christopher Wren's)

Drawing on your knowledge! p53

1 Doom painting
2 Cromwell
3 Hans Holbein
4 Woodcut

Naming names! p53

Isaac Newton
William Harvey
Edmond Halley
Robert Boyle

Woman wise! p57

1 false; she was called a shrew.
2 true.
3 false; they could, but only if there were no close male heirs.
4 false; most women married, however not all.

Schools up! p59

1 <u>Not many</u> children went to school in this period. Some children were educated at home, for example Thomas More's daughters. They had a very <u>good</u> home education.
2 Children could become apprentices instead of going to school. Their masters <u>were allowed</u> to beat them.
3 Children could be married very young, for example, Catherine <u>Howard</u> was <u>15</u> when she married the <u>49</u>-year-old Henry VIII.

Helping the poor? p63

1 vagrant
2 branding
3 enclosure
4 monasteries
5 Elizabethan poor laws

Plaguing puzzles p65

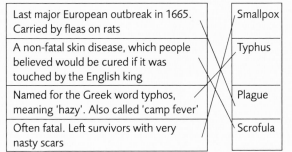

Last major European outbreak in 1665. Carried by fleas on rats	Smallpox
A non-fatal skin disease, which people believed would be cured if it was touched by the English king	Typhus
Named for the Greek word typhos, meaning 'hazy'. Also called 'camp fever'	Plague
Often fatal. Left survivors with very nasty scars	Scrofula

Hangagrams p67

1 Matthew Hopkins
2 Blackbeard
3 Francis Drake
4 Catherine Howard
5 Dick Turpin

Test your knowledge 1

1
1 G	2 K	3 I	4 M	5 L
6 F	7 C	8 B	9 J	10 N
11 D	12 O	13 H	14 E	15 A

2 Yorkist, Tudor, Stuart, Hanoverian
3 Henry VII, Henry VIII, Edward VI, Mary I, Elizabeth I, James I, Charles I, the Protectorate (or the Republic, or the Commonwealth)/Cromwell Cromwell's son, Charles II, James II, William III and Mary II, Anne, George I, George II

Test your knowledge 2

These are suggested answers. You don't have to say everything that's there. You might also have different points to make. If you aren't sure whether your answers are good ones, show them to your teacher.

1 Answers:
   a Jesus
   b the papacy
2 Suggested points to cover in your answer:
   a The papacy (the 'supreme government' of the church 'rightfully belongs to the see of Rome')
   b It was given to the papacy by Jesus himself ('granted by the mouth of our Saviour himself')
3 Suggested points to cover in your answers:
   a The supreme government of the Church belongs to the Pope. 'No more might this realm of England refuse obedience to the see of Rome than might a child refuse obedience to his own natural father.' In other words, Henry should not have declared himself head of the Church.
   b More implies that the court has no right to judge him. This is because its judgement is based on laws that are 'directly hateful to the laws of God and his Holy Church'.
4 Suggested points to cover in your answer:
   • More might be angry because he's been condemned. This might mean he says things he doesn't really mean.
   • On the other hand, it doesn't matter what More says any more – he's going to die in any case. So he can tell the truth and say exactly what he thinks.
5 Suggested points to cover in your answer:
   • Most people were not prepared to be executed for denying that Henry was head of the Church. In fact, almost all of Henry VIII's bishops were prepared to accept him as head of the Church, even though they would have sworn loyalty to the pope when they became bishops. So Thomas More was not typical of most people because he was prepared to die rather than say that Henry was head of the Church.
   • Many people wouldn't have been that bothered about who was head of the Church. They were more bothered about what happened in their own lives. This is perhaps why more people did speak out when Henry started to close the monasteries, because monasteries did matter in their daily lives. (There was a big rebellion in the north of England, called the 'Pilgrimage of Grace', in 1536–37)
   • However, people would have been scared to speak out against Henry, in case they got into trouble. So Thomas More might have been saying what people thought but were too scared to say.

Test your knowledge 3

These are suggested answers. You don't have to say everything that's there. You might also have different points to make. If you aren't sure whether your answers are good ones, show them to your teacher.

1 Possible answers:
   • Luther is very strong – he is able to stand up in front of the whole Diet and refuse to back down ('I will not recant anything'). He is also prepared to go against the papacy ('I do not accept the authority of popes')
   • Luther is very religious ('my conscience is captive to the Word of God'). He also finishes his speech by saying 'Amen', the way that Christians often finish prayers.
   • Luther believes that the Bible is very important (he will not back down unless he is 'convicted by Scripture and plain reason').
   • The source suggests that Luther feels very strongly that he is right. He won't back down ('I will not recant anything') even in front of such an important group of people as the Diet.
   • We get a hint that Luther wants to think for himself, rather than to be told what to think. (He says that he wants to be 'convinced by Scripture and plain reason'). This reminds us that Luther is a university professor.
2 Possible answers:
   • Luther was strong enough to keep to his ideas even when he was under attack. This would have helped to stop him giving up.
   • Someone with such strong ideas might encourage other people to support him – people might have felt they could trust his views because he believed in them.
   • The source suggests that Luther thought and spoke like a university theologian. Perhaps this meant that other theologians would have been more willing to listen to his ideas.
3 Some tips to get you thinking.
   • Think about other reasons for the success of the Reformation. For instance, think about the support of the princes; the popularity of Luther's ideas with people in Germany, or the weaknesses in the Catholic Church.
   • Weigh up all the evidence together. Which is the most important issue? Was it Luther's personality, or was it something else?

Test your knowledge 4

These are some things you might like to think about. You don't have to say everything that's there. You might also have different points to make. If you aren't sure whether your answers are good ones, show them to your teacher.

1 Some things you might like to think about:
   • Parliament getting a bigger role after the Break with Rome because it had to pass a lot of the laws to do with religion.
   • Execution of Charles I.
   • The Glorious Revolution and the Bill of Rights.
   • George I and George II leaving more things to Parliament.

2   Some things you might like to think about:
    • Individual monarchs might have been weaker, but
      that didn't mean that the monarchy was weaker. For
      example, Queen Anne reclaimed a lot of power for
      the Crown.
    • Kings had been deposed a lot in the Middle Ages.
      For example, Richard II had been deposed and
      probably murdered by his nobles. So was the
      monarchy any weaker by 1750 than it had been in
      the Middle Ages?
    • We think of Walpole as the first prime minister.
      However, he didn't have anywhere near as much
      power as our present Prime Minister. The monarchs
      were still in charge of government.
    • The English kings ruled Scotland as well as England,
      and England's government had more power over
      Wales and Scotland.
3   Use your thoughts for questions 1 and 2 to draw your
    own conclusion.

Test your knowledge 5

See the hints in the text.

Test your knowledge 6

See the hints in the text.

Maps

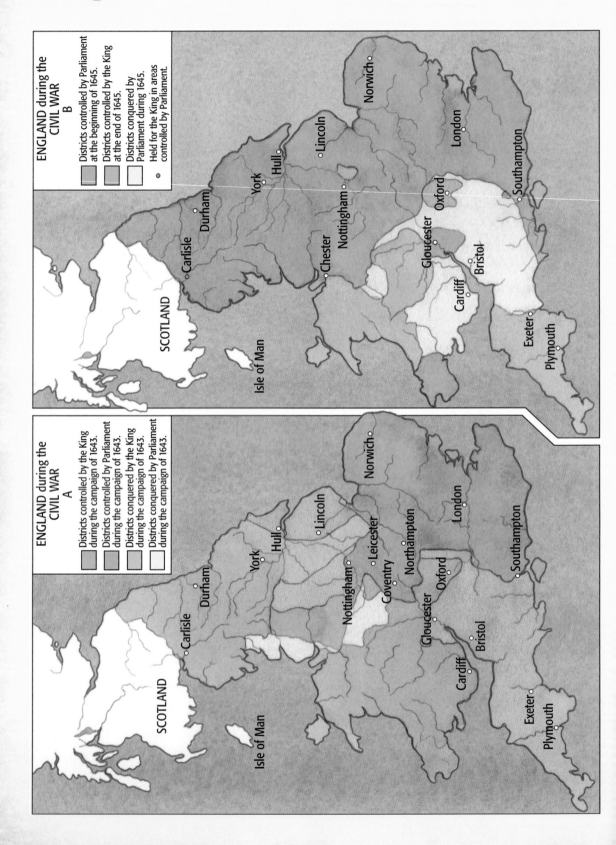

ENGLAND during the CIVIL WAR A

Districts controlled by the King during the campaign of 1643.
Districts controlled by Parliament during the campaign of 1643.
Districts conquered by the King during the campaign of 1643.
Districts conquered by Parliament during the campaign of 1643.

ENGLAND during the CIVIL WAR B

Districts controlled by Parliament at the beginning of 1645.
Districts controlled by the King at the end of 1645.
Districts conquered by Parliament during 1645.
Held for the King in areas controlled by Parliament.

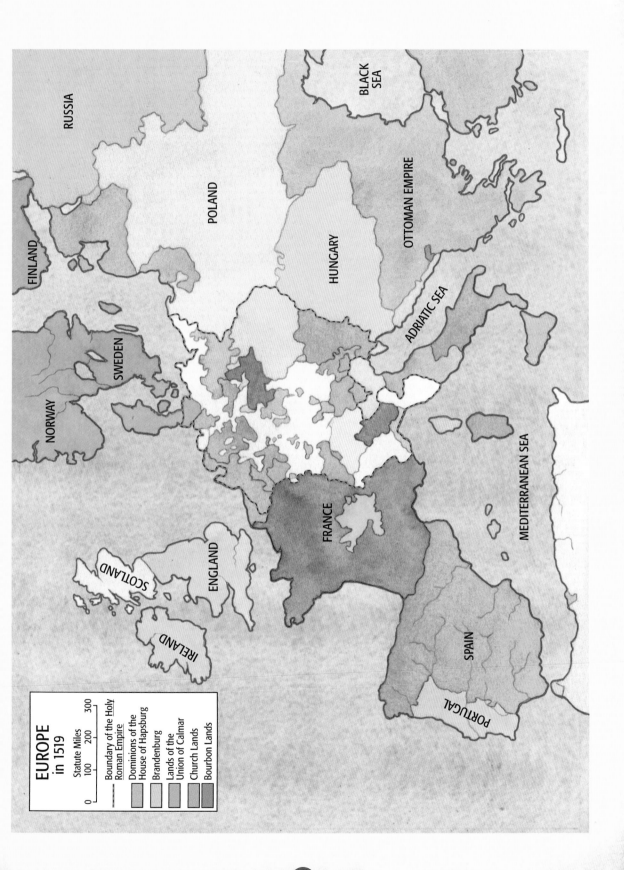

EUROPE
in 1519

Statute Miles
0   100   200   300

Boundary of the Holy
Roman Empire

Dominions of the
House of Hapsburg

Brandenburg

Lands of the
Union of Calmar

Church Lands

Bourbon Lands

FINLAND

RUSSIA

NORWAY

SWEDEN

POLAND

BLACK
SEA

HUNGARY

OTTOMAN EMPIRE

ADRIATIC SEA

SCOTLAND

IRELAND

ENGLAND

FRANCE

SPAIN

PORTUGAL

MEDITERRANEAN SEA

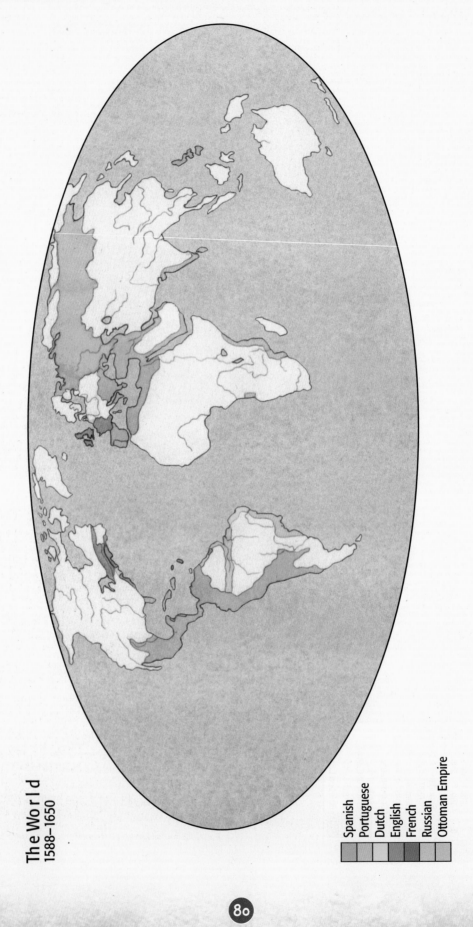

The World
1588–1650

Spanish
Portuguese
Dutch
English
French
Russian
Ottoman Empire